Leaving Home with Faith

LEAVING HOME
WITH FAITH

Nurturing the Spiritual Life of Our Youth

ELIZABETH F. CALDWELL

The Pilgrim Press
Cleveland

The Pilgrim Press, 700 Prospect Avenue East, Cleveland, Ohio 44115-1100
pilgrimpress.com

Grateful acknowledgement for permission to reprint from the following:
Reprinted from *People on the Way: Asian North Americans Discovering Christ, Culture, and Community* edited by David Ng, copyright © 1996 by Judson Press. Used by permission of Judson Press, 800-4-JUDSON, www.judsonpress.com. ❖ Reproduced from *Growing in the Life of Faith* © 1999 Craig Dykstra. Used by permission of Geneva Press. ❖ *Yes, Your Teen is Crazy! Loving Your Kid without Losing Your Mind,* Michael J. Bradley (Gig Harbor, Wash.: Harbor Press, 2002). Used by permission. ❖ From *Secrets of Strong Families* by Nick Stinnett. Copyright © 1985 by Nick Stinnett and John DeFrain. By permission of Little, Brown and Company. (Inc.)

All scripture quotations, unless otherwise indicated, are from the *New Revised Standard Version Bible,* copyright © 1989 by the Division of Christian Education of the National Council of the Churches of Christ in the U.S.A. Used by permission.

Library of Congress Cataloging-in-Publication Data

Caldwell, Elizabeth, 1948-
    Leaving home with faith : nurturing the spiritual life of our youth / Elizabeth F. Caldwell.
        p.   cm.
    Includes bibliographical references.
    ISBN 0-8298-1504-X (pbk. : alk. paper)
    1. Christian education of children. 2. Children—Religious life. 3. Parenting—Religious aspects—Christianity. I. Title.

BV1475.3 .C35   2002
248.8'45—dc21
                                                                2002035477

Contents

Preface 7

1 Living In-Between 13

2 A Faith That Grows 29

3 Good-Enough Parents 47

4 Confirmed and Commissioned: Connecting Faith 67
   and Life

5 A Backpack of Belonging 95

6 Suggestions for Teaching and Resources 113

Appendices 130

Notes 140

Preface

- My wonderful child has turned into someone I don't recognize. Every thing I say or do is questioned or suspect. What kind of parent does she need?

- The questions my teenager is asking about God and faith are not ones I know how to answer. What do I do?

- I'm going to make my son go to confirmation class. I did it when I was his age and so will he. Then he'll know about the Christian faith. After that, he can make his own decisions about church and whether he goes or not.

- My daughter doesn't seem to fit in anywhere at church. She says she doesn't have any friends and doesn't want to go. What do I do?

- I try to be patient with my teenage son and remember what it was like when I was his age. Kids today are growing up in a world that is so different from the one I experienced as a teenager.

Parents of adolescents in these beginning years of the new millennium are raising their children in an era described as postmodern. This label describes a time in which we know there are multiple points of view on every question, in which it is not easy to stake out one standpoint from which to view the world and say, "This is the truth!" In this era, time is measured by the speed of Internet connections and communication is evaluated by the number of connections you have . . . pagers, cell phones, multiple phone lines, digital cables. Adults who grew up in homes with one TV with three or four channels and one phone now raise their children in an environment in which the options seem to be limitless. We live and work with people from different cultural backgrounds and know that words and gestures don't mean the same as they do to us.

When parents of adolescents were children, they faced issues of racism that were embedded in separate and non-equal school systems, a nation at war in Vietnam, and the beginnings of the reality of poverty and sexism and their deeply embedded practices in the culture and in the church. Increasing numbers of countries possessed the capability of using the bomb and the fear of those whose hand controlled the button for weapons capable of destroying the world were not far away from the thinking and concern of adults whose children are now parents of adolescents. Making a long distance call was something you thought about before you picked up the phone and began to dial.

As I write this introduction, the world has changed forever—at least it has from the perspective of those who live in the United States. It is a week after September 11, 2001, the day when the security and peace of our nation was uprooted, and we now know that we live in a time in which the predictable is gone forever. Churches across the nation were filled on Sunday, September 16, to the extent that it looked like the attendance on Easter Sunday, only it wasn't a holiday. In the search for understanding, in the desire for community, in the need for faith to sustain the deepest and darkest questions, people gathered to worship God who is above all time and space.

At a baptism or a dedication of an infant, parents promise to raise their child in faith. Sacraments and liturgical rituals of this kind are opportunities in worship for adults to acknowledge that their journey through parenthood is not solitary but communal. A community of faith covenants to walk with parents and children through all the steps along the way of growth and development and parents acknowledge their trust in God whose sustaining presence will see them through each day of their child's life.

This book is the last in a series of three. I began in 1994 with exploring the meaning of the sacraments of baptism and Holy Communion for parents and congregations in the book *Come unto Me: Rethinking the Sacraments for Children* (Cleveland: United Church Press, 1996). In writing that book and listening to pastors, educators, and parents, I became convinced that the church in its educational programs could not adequately educate children to grow in the life of the Christian faith. It is a partnership between the parents and their family and the church. *Making a Home for Faith: Nurturing the Spiritual Life of Your Children* (Cleveland: The Pilgrim Press, 2000) was written to address the issue of parents as the primary faith educators of children.

One illustration has been the impetus for writing this book. It's a not uncommon voice heard in churches across this country. Pastors speak of parents who send their young adolescents to confirmation to learn everything they will need to know about the Christian faith. Some of these parents have struck a bargain with their teenager that if he or she goes to confirmation class and is confirmed in the church, then participation in the life of the church becomes his or her choice. In this illustration, confirmation becomes graduation from the church. Kids leave and some never return while others come back as young parents seeking help from the church in raising their own children in a Christian faith tradition.

I find that parents who strike this bargain with their teenager do so out of frustration. They are tired of the Sunday morning arguments and so they work out a deal. It's a bad deal. Rather than conceiving of the preposterous notion that faith, life, and Christian identity are contained within the box of a schooling model of instruction called confirmation class, I offer the image of a "backpack of belonging."

A common sight at middle schools and high schools is teenagers getting off school buses and out of cars with their backpacks of books on their shoulders. This backpack represents a symbol of the consistency and changes they are experiencing in their lives. This same backpack that they carried in elementary school is now heavier with bigger books and more homework. It is weighty with concerns about friends, the future, and questions of faith and life.

This book will explore these two themes faced by adolescents, their families, and their congregations. What changes are they experiencing and what are the implications of these changes for those who live and work with them? In the midst of great changes, what consistencies of family, congregational life, and faith are needed to support youth we know and love?

There seem to be two genres of literature helpful in understanding and relating to adolescents. One is written from a developmental or therapeutic perspective to help parents remember the particular needs of youth in this period of the human life cycle and the implications for raising adolescents in our culture. *The Second Family: How Adolescent Power Is Challenging the American Family* by Ron Taffel; *Reviving Ophelia: Saving the Selves of Adolescent Girls* by Mary Pipher; *A Fine Young Man: What Parents, Mentors, and Educators Can Do to Shape Adolescent Boys into Exceptional Men* by Michael Gurian; *Trust Me, Mom—Everyone Else Is Going: The New Rules for Mothering Adolescent Girls* by Roni Cohen-Sandler; and *Yes, Your Teen Is Crazy: Loving Your Kid without Losing Your Mind* by Michael J. Bradley are a few examples.

A second genre of literature is written from a faith perspective for an audience of those engaged in ministry with youth in congregational settings. *The Godbearing Life* by Kenda Creasy Dean and Ron Foster; *Blessing New Voices: Prayers of Young People and Worship Resources for Youth Ministry* by Maren C. Tirabassi; *Pastoral Counseling with Adolescents and Young Adults* by Charles Shelton; and *Career and Calling* by Ginny Ward Holderness and Forest C. Palmer are excellent examples of the kind of educational and pastoral resources available to adults who care about youth in their congregations.

This book is written for parents of younger adolescents, for pastors and educators, and for caring adults and other family members who model the life of the Christian faith, serving as a bridge between these two kinds of writing in its focus on the place where adolescents, parents and family, faith, and the church intersect. It seeks to hold parents accountable to their role as primary faith educators of their teenage child.

Each chapter in this book deals with adolescence from a particular perspective. The first chapter, "Living In-Between" provides a developmental perspective on adolescence, who they are and why, as they make the transition from being children to becoming young adults. Chapter 2, "A Faith That Grows," offers a theological lens for looking at faith issues and teenagers. Chapter 3, "Good-Enough Parents," is written to help parents step back and take a look at the changes in their roles and in the life of their family as their children move into adolescence. Chapter 4, "Confirmed and Commissioned: Connecting Faith and Life," offers an educational perspective for considering the role of the faith community in confirming and commissioning youth in their faith and life. Chapter 5 uses the image of "A Backpack of Belonging" to offer some suggestions for things that youth and parents need to keep accessible in the changes they face together as a family.

One way this book might be used is in a four-to-six-week, adult, short-term class for parents of older children and youth. Discussion questions included in chapter six are written to facilitate such a discussion. Included with each chapter is a brief reflection on a psalm. This collection of songs of praise helps us learn ways we can come to God as individual persons and as community. Including time for prayer and engagement with a psalm while thinking about the faith of adolescents, families, and congregations is a way to affirm the essential relationship between biblical study and growing in the life of the Christian faith.

From the moment of adoption or birth into a family of faith, parents, grandparents, aunts, uncles, siblings, and the church contribute to the nurturing of a child's life of faith. Prayers, reading the Bible, sharing with others, worshiping together, struggling to understand the deepest questions of life and faith—these faithful acts are added to a backpack of belonging. This metaphor is used to illustrate the cumulative nature of experiences that enable parents to remember and affirm their work over the lifetime of their child, their commitment to enabling this young life to know and experience what it means to belong to God, to belong to a family, and to belong to the life of a community of faith.

This book could not have been written without the help and support of a number of people. I wrote a major part of this book while living in Nashville with my sister and her family. They welcomed me into their home and lives and into the life of their congregation and for that I am forever grateful. McCormick Theological Seminary generously provided me with sabbatical time to research and write this book and James Hudnut-Beumler, dean of the divinity school at Vanderbilt University, welcomed me with a space for reading and writing in the library.

Second Presbyterian Church in Nashville, Tennessee, gave me the opportunity to write, design, and teach confirmation with a group of seventh and eighth graders. I joined a teaching team and we journeyed through this together. It was not without some measure of anxiety that I jumped in with younger adolescents, wondering if, after eighteen years of teaching adults, I could switch gears. Spending eight months with dedicated teachers, eighteen mentors, and eighteen teenagers was truly incredible. So thanks to Stacy Rector, associate pastor of Second Presbyterian Church and Cathy Hoop, director of children's ministry who made this possible. Gordon Brewer and Kristen Denmon welcomed me as a coteacher and Bailey Williams, Jacob McNutt, Tory Adcock, Josh Hoop, Katy Brantley, Kelly Dennison, Skyler Moots, Andrew Tumen, Bobby Goodrich, Callie Jennings, Amy Dixon, Katherine Lea, John Early, Nathan Sears, Spence Hobson, Mary Katherine Batson, Steve Leonard-Martin, and Newton Allen helped me remember how to teach teenagers. Their curiosity, enthusiasm, and variety of gifts of the spirit challenged and inspired me.

As I left our confirmation class each Sunday morning and walked to the sanctuary, I thought about the lesson plan and how it had worked out in the actual teaching. I recalled comments made by the youth, and in the spring, toward the end of the class, I reflected on the beginning and how individual persons came together in a community of learning, sharing, and living the Christian faith. As you teach or live, talk, work, or walk with a teenager, be sure that the resources in your own backpack of faith and belonging are sufficient for the journey.

Living In-Between

Seventh and eighth graders arrive for church school on a Sunday morning. Watching them walk into the room and listening to their conversations and seeing the ways they relate to one another (or not) is a fascinating exercise. In addition to ranges of styles of dress, from extremely casual to dressier pants or skirts and blouses, their bodies give evidence of the changes taking place internally. In any given group of twelve-to-fourteen year olds, you can find a wide range of physical, mental, and social development.

Physical growth for some is three-fourths of the way to maturity, while for others it has not yet begun. Adults willing to teach youth in church school or to work with them in other forms of ministry (youth groups, mission trips, mentoring programs) receive great blessings from parents, "Thanks for caring about my teenager. It means a lot that another adult thinks he is an okay person." Others in the church view these same adults with a different kind of gratitude: "I'm glad you're willing to teach them; I could never do that. Give me a college-age student any time." "I love teaching young children, but I know I could never teach teenagers. I don't know how you do it!" One adolescent has observed, "People look at teenagers like we're a totally alien life-form."[1]

Occasionally, parents switch into a survivor mentality. When comparing stories with parents of other adolescents, they gain a sense of the commonality of the issues that they are facing in the changes in their children. Sometimes shared stories remind them that their situation is certainly not as bad as others. A teenager with a mouth that talks back is very different from a teenager who is starving herself to death.

There are two conceptions of adolescence. One addresses the issue of the changes that an adolescent is experiencing, changes that mark their transition from being a child to becoming a young adult. Mary Pipher has said that:

> Adolescence is a border between adulthood and childhood and as such it has a richness and a diversity unmatched by any other life stage. . . . With adolescence, many kinds of development occur—physical, emotional, intellectual, academic, social and spiritual—and they don't always occur in tandem. . . . Puberty is defined as a biological process, while adolescence is defined as the social and personal experience of that process.[2]

Lyn Mikel Brown and Carol Gilligan have studied the transition of girls into adolescence. They frame the issue of this border time in terms of the risks they experience. "For girls at adolescence to say what they are feeling and thinking often means to risk, in the words of many girls, losing their relationships and finding themselves powerless and all alone."[3] The challenge to parents is to know how to respond to all the changes being experienced by their child.

A second conception of adolescence focuses on the effects of these developmental changes. Wade Rowatt describes adolescence as a long time of preparation, essential for living independently. "Adolescence, a recent development, reflects the long drawn-out time needed to prepare for independent living. . . . Teens have adult bodies and expanded brains but they have no adult roles."[4]

This period in the human life-cycle is, as Rowatt observes, a more recent addition to our understanding of human development. As our nation moved from a primarily agrarian society to face the changes of the industrial revolution in the nineteenth century, occupations required greater degrees of advanced skills. Adolescent sons and daughters no longer left school to work on the farm. The period between childhood and adulthood assumed a life of its own as one of education and preparation to assume the mantle of adulthood.

The title of David Elkind's book, *All Grown Up and No Place to Go,* captures the tension present in this border time between developed bodies, developing brains, and the lack of place or role in the culture for adolescents.[5] With bodies and brains changing and developing, it's no wonder that adolescents feel they are a "totally alien life-form," not children and not yet adults. With minds capable of abstract thinking and bodies fully developed, yet having brains still being wired for controls related to emotions, impulse restraint, and rational decision-making, it does seem a miracle that many make it through unscathed.

The consistent issue of adolescent development is that of change. Parents, and those who work with youth, know experientially the issues of developmental theory. You see and live with the physical and emotional changes of teenagers. The challenge for parents, and those who teach and are in ministry with adolescents, is understanding and knowing how to be consistent in relationship with young people and all the changes they are experiencing in their physical self, emotional self, academic self, social self (with family and with peers) and spiritual self.[6]

Parents of adolescents went through the same physical and mental changes. What is different for today's adolescents is the world in which we live, a world of Internet chat rooms, life-style options, a world that is increasingly more violent and dangerous, a world where ethical decisions are faced on a daily basis, a world filled with a diversity of culture and faith traditions. To go through these kinds of changes is, as Brown and Gilligan suggest, a risk.

Both of these positive understandings of adolescence help remind those who live with, teach, or work with youth that the effort to communicate, stay in relationship, and love them even when they aren't so lovable is essential for healthy adolescent growth and development.

This chapter will give you an overview of developmental theorists' perspective on adolescence. This perspective provides a framework for understanding the fluid nature of a young person's development. The chapter will conclude with some thoughts about the implications of these changes for those who live with, teach, and are in ministry with teenagers.

Some Myths and Realities of Adolescence

Over twenty years ago an educator contrasted the realities of adolescent development with five myths that she believed represented popular cultural thinking about teenagers. Joan Scheff Lipsitz wrote that she believed our culture responded to teenagers out of the myths of believing that adolescence, rather than being a normal time of development in the human life span, was instead a pathological time. Other myths she believed were at work in the culture were that adolescents should be regarded as all alike, a homogeneous group, a group that really should be treated as children, and a group from which the culture can expect uniform and fairly continuous growth. The fifth myth regarding this time in the life span was that adolescence is really just a transitional time in their life.[7]

The realities of this time of development are that it is as normal as any other time in the life span. To expect a group of adolescents to be alike just because they are near each other in age is to deny the variability of this age group. Change and growth—biological, intellectual, social, and emotional—is a normal expectation, but synchronized change is not reasonable to assume.

Perhaps the statement that adolescents are children is the one myth no longer prevalent in our understandings of this age group. A more accurate myth is the one that says, "Youth are almost adults and will do okay if we just let them alone." Too many youth are literally left alone, unattended by parents, taking care of themselves:

> The here and now is at no time in our lives more intensely experienced than when we are adolescents. What we are saying to too many young people is, "Be good, have fun, stay out of trouble, prepare for life, and we'll get back to you later when we like you better and understand you more."[8]

One point could be added to the myth of homogeneity of this age group. Adolescent development for females and males shares some similarities but also has clearly identified differences. Research and writings that focus on cultural expectations for what it means to be a female or a male have contributed to our understanding of what is necessary for being a parent of daughters and sons. Consider the complexity of this issue of identity from the perspective of three educators:

> Something dramatic happens to girls in early adolescence. Just as planes and ships disappear mysteriously into the Bermuda Triangle, so do the selves of girls go down in droves. They crash and burn in a social and developmental Bermuda Triangle.[9]

Mary Pipher is speaking of the transition some adolescent girls experience when they face the issue of being faithful to themselves or of being socially acceptable. This time, Pipher believes, is one when "girls learn to be nice rather than honest." She says in her work as a therapist, she has identified four ways that adolescent girls react to the pressures in the culture to abandon the self and to the growing realization that the world has been established with male norms. "They can conform, withdraw, be depressed or get angry."[10] Research into the lives of adolescent girls by Mary Pipher and Lyn Mikel Brown and Carol Gilligan has shown that oftentimes the face they offer to the world is the answer, "I don't know." In speaking about adolescence, Gilligan and Brown's research has seen evidence of

loss of voice, a struggle to authorize or take seriously their own experience—to listen to their feelings and thoughts—increased confusion, sometimes defensiveness, as well as evidence for the replacement of real with inauthentic or idealized relationships.[11]

The second example illustrates a male issue:

The boy code is a set of behaviors, rules of conduct, cultural shibboleths, and even a lexicon, that is inculcated into boys by our society—from the very beginning of a boy's life. In effect we hold up a mirror to our boys that reflects back a distorted and outmoded image of the ideal boy—an image that our boys feel under great pressure to emulate.[12]

Pollack suggests that, for boys, the code is "everything is just fine," which he believes is a "mask of masculinity," encouraging boys to communicate to the world, "I can handle it. Everything's fine. I am invincible."[13]

To say that adolescence is a time of transition implies that if we just wait long enough, they will pass through it and everything will be okay again. What do we do as parents, teachers, pastors with youth?

In her book, *Act Your Age! A Cultural Construction of Adolescence*, Nancy Lesko argues for a different conception of adolescence, one that recognizes their abilities to be responsible contributors to society:

Typically teenagers appear in our cultural talk as synonymous with crazed hormones, as delinquents, deficiencies, or clowns, that is, beings not to be taken too seriously. They are most often spoken of with familiarity, sometimes with affection, and regularly with some hostility or displeasure. In these various venues and with decidedly mixed emotions, we talk about "the trouble with teenagers."[14]

Lesko's comments suggest one additional myth of adolescence. It is the myth that once you are through adolescence, life will become more stable, less dominated by change. The reality of life is change. We are always in the process of growing, becoming, until the moment when our lives are over. This is also Lesko's argument that youth and adults alike are in the process of becoming. Lesko believes that by assigning youth to a period of waiting and watching them as they become developmentally mature, we have condemned them to "an 'expectant time'— a moratorium of responsibility and of power."[15]

Consider the ways that these myths may be alive and well in the attitudes and actions of your congregation. In what ways does the church welcome teenagers, affirm them, and invite their presence and leadership?

Thinking Developmentally

Wade Rowatt writes:

> The building blocks of personality such as trust, autonomy, initiative, and industry become set during childhood. Work attitudes, intimacy styles, and self-image normally grow naturally through the teen years. However, adolescence represents a second chance for teens to revisit earlier, childhood issues and then reach mature development.[16]

A way to begin to understand some of the realities of this time in the human lifecycle is to view adolescence in terms of four stages of development: Pre-Adolescence—Ages 10–12; Early Adolescence—Ages 12–14; Middle Adolescence—Ages 15–17; and Late Adolescence—Ages 18–19.

Six theorists, educators, and therapists provide frameworks for understanding the realities and potential resident within this time in the human life span. The first four speak from within the conceptual framework of human development. Erik Erikson's research has given us a theory of the psychosocial development of humans. During adolescence, two tensions are being resolved: identity or role confusion and intimacy or isolation. In Erikson's theory, which is based on research with males, these two developmental tasks are sequential. Self-definition, or the establishment of identity, precedes self-connection or the capacity for intimate relations.

Carol Gilligan's research adds an important voice in understanding the particular challenges faced by female adolescents in this culture and raises the question of the viability of Erikson's sequential steps in psychosocial development. She questions whether the developmental task of intimacy (especially for adolescent women) coincides with the task of identity formation rather than following it as suggested in Erikson's research with males. Intimacy involves the ability to make commitments to another and to live with the consequences of those commitments, consequences such as sacrifice and compromise. Intimacy also implies the ability to be close to another emotionally or physically, to share confidences, private thoughts, and feelings with another.

I find that Robert Kegan's writing about human growth in terms of the two lifelong tasks of integrating and separating to be helpful. Rather than viewing these as sequential developmental tasks, Kegan understands that development as a human being involves a constant movement between individuation, becoming a self and connecting and relating to and with others. Kegan provides a bridge between the developmental theorists and educators who deal with learning and cognition. For Kegan, the establishment of an identity, the chance for self-definition is a critical task of adolescence. And truly adolescents are "a work in progress" so to speak as they begin the essential task that enables their healthy journey to adulthood, the construction of their own unique self.

A parent went to a conference at school with the teachers of his thirteen-year-old son. The teachers talked about his son's abilities in reading, writing, and social studies, and his father said that would be expected in their family because it was a value and interest on both sides of the family. Then the teachers asked about the adolescent's interest in math and science, rockets and robots and his father laughed and said, "We don't know where that comes from, certainly not from me!"

This is an age of the identification of interests and passions, the formation of a self that may share or diverge from those of their parents. If you were to look closely at a group of young adolescents (ages twelve to fourteen), you would see a wide continuum represented in those who are working on issues of identity and intimacy. Think about the differences you observe in such a group of young adolescents. What factors contribute to this difference—birth order, being male and female, family dynamics, school culture, peer influence, physical development?

In his book *Pastoral Counseling with Adolescents and Young Adults*, Charles Shelton has included a diagram that helps to visually present the process of an adolescent's formation of her or his own self. In this diagram, the younger adolescent has a fairly fragile identity, not yet capable of standing on its own. Shelton notes that peers help to fill in the gaps, providing "a protective shell needed to bolster the adolescent's fragile sense of self."[17]

In middle adolescence and the transition to late adolescence, more of the structure of the individual is in place as the young person is capable of more autonomy and strong friendships, one-on-one. Shelton reminds us that the developmental task of forming an identity is a process, something youth grow into through the stages of early, middle, and late adolescence. His clinical and pastoral work with adolescents has enabled his development of a list of healthy characteristics of this age group. This list can be used by parents or those who work with youth in the church to determine how healthy development is progressing in the adolescents' lives. See Appendix 1 for a list of these characteristics.

When your teenager begins spending more time in his room, Shelton believes that this is a healthy development of an adolescent's ability to be comfortable with solitude and with his sense of who he is. Another healthy characteristic on Shelton's list is a growing capacity for complex thinking that is more akin to the thinking of adults than it is to older elementary age children. This has important implications for the ways in which a church plans for the Christian education of adolescents.

Shelton's checklist of personality characteristics to watch for in maturing adolescents is useful for parents and those who work with youth in the church. The glimmer of some of these traits is apparent in younger adolescents and becomes more fully evident in older adolescents. Families play a key role in nurturing these abilities. For example, the ability to accept yourself in terms of identity and in accepting physical changes is difficult when parents expect perfection.

Two educational theorists offer insights into how the developing human is supported in learning. Writing in Russia in the early part of the twentieth century, L.S. Vygotsky described a zone of proximal development that he believed

> defines those functions that have not yet matured but are in the process of maturation, functions that will mature tomorrow but

are currently in an embryonic state. These functions could be termed the "buds" or "flowers" of development rather than the "fruits" of development. The actual developmental level characterizes mental development retrospectively, while the zone of proximal development characterizes mental development prospectively.[18]

Another twentieth-century educator, Jerome Bruner, speaks of the activity of "scaffolding," which is a connecting link or activity provided by a peer or an adult for a person who is pushing against the boundaries of their own abilities. Parents know the importance of supporting and encouraging their child's social relationships. Play dates and having friends over after school, activities that begin in preschool and continue through elementary years are essential building blocks for children in learning how to be a friend and how to keep friends. Some parents know that for any number of reasons, it may not be easy for their child to do this. So, knowing this, parents encourage and support and, in some ways, gently nudge their child into a zone of proximal development of social skills. They become a bridge or as Bruner would say, they provide a scaffold. For an introverted or less socially adept teenager, wise parents continue to gently nurture and encourage this development in their child. Finally, recent work with brain development offers insight into the behaviors of adolescence that are sometimes difficult to understand.

Up until now, psychologists had a lot of great sounding theories to explain why adolescents tend to act so crazy at times. We believed that all that risk-taking, judgment-impaired, aggressive and oppositional behavior was a function of early childhood experiences, peer pressure, the hormonal effects of puberty, and, most hurtful of all for too many mothers and fathers, poor parenting. No one thought that massive structural changes in teenagers' brains were largely to blame. We had no clue that their brains were changing.[19]

In his book *Yes, Your Teen is Crazy! Loving Your Kid without Losing Your Mind,* Michael J. Bradley goes on to say that brain research has helped us understand that ninety-five percent of the brain is developed by the time a child is five years old. Recent research from the National Institute of Mental Health on how a child's brain develops between the ages of three and eighteen has shown that the more advanced parts of the brain in the prefrontal cortex experience a time of growth during adolescence. Researchers have found that emotional control, restraint of impulses, and rational decision-making abilities reside in this part of the brain. It "does the bulk of its maturation between the ages of twelve and twenty. The prefrontal cortex is where the most sophisticated of our abilities reside."[20] One researcher has described this part of the brain as "the seat of civilization," that part of ourselves that enables us both to live with ourselves and to function in community.

These last three educators remind us of the role of adults in the lives of adolescents, no matter where they are within the borders of that time of development—pre, early, middle, or late adolescence. Their healthy movement within this time of life is enabled by caring adults who are able to affirm where they are, yet at the same time see the implicit potential for new development, new discoveries of identity, and the capacities for relationships.

An ecological perspective on adolescent development is more complete when viewed through the lens of these therapists, educators, and developmental theorists. Their research enables us not only to understand the markers of this time in the human life cycle but also to provide us with clues about the role of adults in supporting and enabling a healthy movement from childhood to adolescence and then into adulthood.

At the beginning of this section is a quote from Wade Rowatt that is important to remember. Adolescents are not starting over. As Rowatt suggests, the building blocks of their personality are in place. This is a time in life when they begin to make the connections between the blocks and how they impact their own individual development. His image of a "second chance" is important to remember for adults who live with the emotional ups and downs of growing adolescents.

A Bridge through Adolescence

The title of this chapter suggests the experiences of both adolescents and those who live with them and are in ministry with them. As the literal meaning of the word "adolescence" suggests, they are on their way to becoming less of a child and more of an adult—from the Latin *adolescere*, to grow up.

What enables their healthy movement through adolescence? Parents and teachers know that it is a combination of two qualities: expectation and comfort or support. Finding the right balance between these is essential. Parents have been balancing these qualities since the birth or adoption of their child, holding them accountable and responsible to themselves and their abilities and offering the kind of nurture that assures a child that in experiences of success and failure, they are loved.

Robert Kegan has described the self as being embedded in an environment that has three functions: holding on, letting go, and remaining in place. It is a reality of transformation that continues as we deal with changes we face throughout our life. He believes that when adults support an adolescent, they are providing the kind of healthy holding environment that "fosters developmental transformation or the process by which the whole ("how I am") becomes gradually a part ("how I was") of a new whole ("how I am now).[21]

Essential for a teenager is the image of a bridge that, if it is to support the healthy transformation of an adolescent, must be firmly anchored on both ends as she or he moves between childhood and becoming a young adult: "People grow best where they continuously experience an ingenious blend of support and challenge."[22]

Balanced with the reality of the consistency of change in all areas of their life, adolescents need a bridge of consistency in their lives. For those who live with, teach, and are in ministry with teenagers, it is essential to appreciate the variety, support a sense of balance in their lives, and provide time.

The other side of the myth of homogeneity of adolescents mentioned earlier in this chapter is the reality of the great variety present within any group of adolescents. One way to gain a sense of this variety is to notice teenagers at church, how they interact with one another and who stands alone, apart from the group. As has been mentioned in this chapter, there is the consistency of growth in this age group as well as a consistency in difference among them.

The world of the adolescent is filled with a variety of people who love them, teach them, and serve as role models, people who are not their parent or parents. When you watch your teenage daughter have a conversation at church with the adult who was present at her baptism, you give a silent prayer of thanksgiving that you are not alone in nurturing this person in faith. Other faithful adults, teachers, youth group leaders, pastors, confirmation mentors are visible examples of the "cloud of witnesses" (Heb. 12:1) that both challenge and support an adolescent's journey in faith.

A church member told the story of the Maundy Thursday meal and worship at her church that included the ritual of foot-washing. With tears in her eyes, she described the experience of washing the feet of a teenager, one she had taught as a preschooler. Having been part of his life as one of his teachers when he was very young, she had the opportunity in a very different setting to care for him in a new way, to take water and a towel and to look in his eyes and remember a much smaller child and to give thanks for his life, raised in a community of faith.

When a child is welcomed into a family through birth or adoption, adults gather around, looking at this child and wondering whom she or he will become. What will he be like? What interests will she have? The answers to those questions evolve over the years of a child's development so that as adolescence begins, we see a variety of expressions of self, some particularly unique to the individual and some shared with others in the family. The unique person a teenager is becoming presents a challenge to a parent or parents as they consider the variety of opportunities available for an adolescent's pursuit of study and vocation. Wise parents help their developing adolescent balance honoring the present and looking to the future that is ahead of them.

With the reality of change being the constant in their lives, adolescents need the consistent support of balance in their lives. Parents can help them acknowledge and implement this balance. Teenagers experiencing a spurt of physical growth need a balance between their busy life of school, friends, and activities and time for being and resting. Weekends become time for catch up on sleep, rest that restores a busy and involved life. As time spent with friends after school and on weekends grows in importance, as well as the need for solitude, parents can help adolescents seek a balance with time for family—meals together, special weekly or monthly family activities.

Parents are aware of the delicate balance that they have been negotiating through the life of their child, knowing when to care for them and help them and when to honor their independence, their ability to make their way on their own. We hope parents have also been helping their child experience a balance between receiving and giving. These values become even more important in adolescence as the expectations for time in their life becomes as demanding as for adults. The actions of parents who model a balance of time for work, rest, play, meditation, and participation in the life of a faithful congregation speak louder than words.

For many in this culture, time has truly become our most treasured and protected possession. For families with a parent or parents who work outside the home, finding time to get it all done—keeping up with teenage schedules--school, after-school activities, time for friends, and time for church, not to mention the work required to maintain a home, means that extra time and the way in which it is used is considered very carefully. Families that work together inside the home as well as play together are communicating values about how time is used and how work is shared.

A parent's commitment to be present in the lives of their adolescent, to make time for listening and dialogue, for checking in, is one of those anchors that supports the bridge toward healthy development. One of the joys of watching a child grow in adolescence is the chance to step back, taking some time to observe the person they have become.

Building a bridge of consistency, appreciating the variety present within any group of teenagers, supporting their growth with a priority for providing balance and time are simple and necessary things adults can do that will help youth safely arrive on the other side of becoming a young adult.

When I think about the bridge we are building with adolescents, some implications for congregational ministry emerge. Consider these questions in light of your congregation and its commitment to ministry with and by adolescents:

1. In what ways does your church provide opportunities for youth to be involved in the life and mission of the congregation? Examine your congregation's approach or philosophy of congregational ministry with all ages of youth. Which programs separate youth by age? Which programs integrate and involve them with the rest of the congregation in terms of their abilities, skills, and interests?

2. Youth are developing many skills and talents. For some it is music, for others, sports, still others have excellent technical abilities. Just as with any group of adults, there are youth who have great extroverted interpersonal skills and others who are quieter and more introverted.

In what ways does the church invite the sharing of the time and talents of its youth? How are their interests and abilities welcomed and used at times other than "Youth Sunday"?

3. What pastoral care is available to youth and their parents? Struggles with identity, pressures to succeed, sexual identity, eating disorders, addictions, and mental health are sometimes well hidden within the family and other times are known within a community of faith. It is important for pastors to be in touch with and available to adolescents and families who may need help with referrals for counseling and or therapy.

Teachers and leaders of youth and pastors can be prepared for identifying destructive or unhealthy adolescent behaviors if they have been educated by spending time reading or working with professionals. Consider getting together teachers and leaders of youth in the late summer before the beginning of church school and programs of youth ministry for a time to get to know one another and to become familiar with the adolescents with whom they will be in ministry.

The reality of adolescence is how quickly they are growing and how soon will come the time when they graduate from high school and leave home. The time spent with them in these years supporting their particular interests and gifts and the time spent together as a family and a congregation add to the memories included in their "backpack of belonging."

Psalms for Living In-Between—Psalm 46

Each chapter in this book concludes with reflection on a psalm. I find that the lectionary texts used in worship on Sunday morning and the chance to read the Gospels nurture and sustain my continuing growth as a Christian. Biblical texts are heard, seen, and experienced in word, music, art, and the sacraments in worship and through the lives of people in the congregation.

However, on a daily basis, I usually turn to the Psalms for reading and meditation. I love poetry, and the hymns of the various Psalm writers speak to almost every experience of life. It's amazing that such ancient poetry is timeless. Biblical scholar Bernhard Anderson has said,

"Because the psalmists speak poetically they speak to us—and for us. The deep within them calls out to the deep within us. They articulate the human cry of every person 'out of the depths.'"[23]

Psalm 46 is an excellent illustration of a song of Zion, which was understood as "the historical center around which is gathered the people of God, whose membership is determined by God's choosing, not by human standards."[24]

As you read the psalm, listen for the expressions of the psalmist that articulate the ways God's rule and presence is centered in and with God's people. Make note of the adjectives used to describe God. Take a few minutes and sit with this psalm. Think about teenagers you know. Recall your own experiences as you moved from being a child to being a teenager. What bridges of support were in place for you? What "works of the Lord' are present in your life today? In verse 10, the psalmist writes, "Be still and know that I am God!"

Take time for some sitting, some stillness with this psalm. You may be interested in reading this psalm in the form of prayer that is called *lecto divina* or "divine reading." Read the psalm three times slowly. During the first reading think about a single word that captures the meaning of the psalm. Then, after the second reading, articulate a phrase that summarizes the meaning of the psalm. After reading the psalm for the third time, spend some moments in reflection on the ways God is speaking to you through this psalm. What are you being asked to do? Use this third reflection to lead you into a time of prayer.

leaving home with
Those wh
where t
I
Fos
w

A Faith That Grows

A confirmation class was beginning a study of the Trinity with a month's focus on God—who God is as revealed in scripture, how we understand the nature of God, and the roles of God in the world. Four pieces of newsprint, markers, and watercolors invited responses from seventh and eighth graders to these open-ended sentences:

- God is like . . . a river, a parent, an ocean, a farmer, a king, a shepherd.

- Dear God, why . . . do people suffer? aren't my prayers answered? is there pain? is there evil in the world? is there crime? Where do we really come from?

- I think about God when . . . I walk, talk, live; I see babies; important things happen; I see the outside and creation; I'm at church; there are moments of silence or I'm upset.

- God is . . . neither male nor female; a spirit; not who we think; a friend everywhere; mysterious; everywhere.

The crossing over of the boundary from childhood to adolescence is marked by changes in faith perspective. Questions and wonderings about the mystery and activity of God in the world and in our lives are articulated with deep passion. Basic tenets of faith are, for some adolescents, firmly in place and for others, open to question and examination.

o live with, teach, or are pastor with youth struggle to know
o begin, what to say.

their book *The Godbearing Life*, Kenda Creasy Dean and Ron
er address the issue of honoring the faith perspective of adolescents
en they say that:

> Theology is not an "added ingredient" that we adults are called
> to layer over the experience of youth like so many croutons.
> Young people see the entire fabric of their existence as a theo-
> logical tapestry, the dramatic story of their desire for a God
> who cares enough for them to ask some-thing of them. It is a
> search not only for a God to believe in but also for a God who
> believes in them."[1]

Children come to know God as revealed through the stories of the
lives of people like Miriam and Moses, David and Esther, Ruth,
Naomi and Abraham. The work of Jesus as Son and Savior who healed
women and men, called disciples to follow and teach, the one who broke
laws and asked difficult questions about justice and love, equality, and
ethics is known to youth through the stories they have studied in church
school and through their experiences with older youth and adults in
their congregation. Now, even more than as a child, adolescents are able
to make connections between biblical stories and faith, between the calls
and expectations to characters in biblical stories and expectations for
the ways Christians today are to live in the world.

As youth move through adolescence, their questions are deeper and
the understandings and experiences of God need to be able to grow with
them. Kathleen Norris expresses her own experience in moving into
adolescence and what happened to her faith:

> I have lately realized that what went wrong for me in my Chris-
> tian upbringing is centered in the belief that one had to be
> dressed up, both outwardly and inwardly, to meet God, the
> insidious notion that I need be a firm and even cheerful be-
> liever before I dare show my face in "His" church. Such a God
> was of little use to me in adolescence, and like many women of
> my generation I simply stopped going to church when I could
> no longer be "good," which for girls especially meant not break-
> ing rules, not giving voice to anger or resentment, and not com-
> plaining.[2]

What face of God do we offer to our teenagers? This question, of course, leads to a prior one, what are the beliefs and the faith of parents, teachers, and leaders of youth? And what of the mystery of God as Creator, Redeemer and Sustainer, or Spirit do we explore, open up with teenagers? What do teenagers know of God through watching and living with their parents and family? How are the teachings of Jesus made explicit in the life and mission of their church? Where is the face of God revealed? Where is it hidden?

In his book *Growing Up Religious: Christians and Jews and Their Journeys of Faith*, Robert Wuthnow shares the results of interviews with two hundred adults about their upbringing, the religious practices of their parents and where their faith has led them. He says that for many families, spirituality came to be understood as a way of life, and it did so because

> people grew up living it. The parents, teachers, and clergy who understood this best were the ones who created an environment in which spirituality was fully and deeply embedded. They honored the spirituality of chicken dinners, of gefilte fish, of family Bibles, and of stained-glass windows. . . . Growing up religious also teaches an important lesson about how to live in an increasingly diverse society.[3]

In families where faith was important, it became like a tapestry, woven into their way of life at home and in their commitments to participation in the life of a faith community.

Wuthow's research confirms what we know but rarely state. We grow up religious in simple everyday ways of singing and saying grace at mealtimes, of sending kids off to school with a blessing, "Have a good day, give a good day" or ending the day with the question, "Where did you see God today?" We grow up religious in homes in which helping others, sharing food, and acts of kindness are practiced. We grow up religious in homes in which sabbath candles are lit at Friday evening Shabbat, where Advent candles are lit, one each Sunday of Advent. We grow up religious learning to say prayers, sometimes aloud and sometimes silently. We grow up religious in honoring a liturgical calendar and the movement between seasons of Advent, Christmas, Epiphany, Lent, Easter, and Pentecost.

The previous chapter focused on the changes that are visible in the growth of an adolescent—physical, social, intellectual, and emotional. This chapter focuses on the ways a teenager matures in faith, the "spiritual self" as referred to by Mary Pipher.

In a form similar to the last chapter, the first concept to be considered is growth in faith from the perspective of a variety of educators. Then implications for parenting and teaching adolescents will be addressed. Finally, practical suggestions for spiritual practices will be identified, ones that can sustain a life of faith across the ages.

A Home for Faith

In my previous book, *Making a Home for Faith: Nurturing the Spiritual Life of Your Children*, I explored the role of parents as faith educators, partners with the church in enabling a child's living and growing in the life of the Christian faith. Parents model for their young children what faith is in their words and more importantly in their actions. Since writing that book, I have been curious about what happens next with these children as they move into adolescence. What practices of faith carry over with them? What traditions do families continue to celebrate in the home? What things change as families grow older together? If participation in the life of a congregation is not a commitment of the whole family, what happens at adolescence? In what ways does the role of a parent as a faith educator evolve as children move into adolescence?

In *Making a Home for Faith*, I argued for the importance of the home as a place where faith is nurtured and supported. Wuthnow's research confirms some of my own more limited research and observation. He discovered in the stories the interviewees told about their childhood: "They assimilated religion more by osmosis than by instruction. The act of praying was more important than the content of their petitions. Being in Sunday school was more memorable than anything they may have been taught. Fried chicken or seders or statues of Mary provided the texture of their spiritual understanding."[4]

This conclusion from their study raises interesting questions about teaching, learning, and living the faith. It also raises questions about what will happen if religious formation in the home continues to decline. What is the result of parents who give over the responsibility for their child's "growing up religious" to the church? What happens to youth who grow up being dropped off at church for church school and worship while their parent or parents go out to get coffee?

Reading the chapter "The Sacred at Home" in Wuthnow's book brings to mind these conversations and stories:

- We don't really do a lot at home, other than a blessing at the meal. And sometimes we forget that. When the kids were little, we used to enjoy singing the blessing but now that the kids are teenagers, we've kind of stopped doing that and now I'm not sure what to do.

- It was the beginning of Lent and a teenager's family tradition was to go to church for Ash Wednesday services. He had a lot of homework that night. He told his father he would get it done because he didn't want to miss church.

- We manage to get to church about twice a month. We're out of town at least one weekend a month. My daughter and son go to church school while we go to worship. It's really all we have time for.

- My son really doesn't want to go to church school or worship. He says it's boring. Of course, he also wonders why he has to go when his father doesn't.

- A teenager called his pastor to say he wouldn't be able to be at youth group on Sunday evening because it was the first Sunday in Advent and they always put up their nativity together as a family.

- It's important in our family to keep alive our family and faith traditions—blessings at meals when we all sit down together, keeping a once-a-month family night, lighting the Advent wreath, going to church on Ash Wednesday to mark the beginning of Lent, and volunteering as a family in mission and ministry opportunities of our church.

As she experienced the transition from the life of a poet in New York City to living on family land in South Dakota, Kathleen Norris described it this way. "This is my spiritual geography, the place where I've wrestled my story out of the circumstances of landscape and inheritance. The word 'geography' derives from the Greek words for earth, and writing about Dakota has been a means of understanding that inheritance and reclaiming the holy in it."[5]

Some adolescents are raised in homes in which a spiritual landscape is as natural as breathing. The spiritual geography of others may be meager, sporadic, or even nonexistent. Adolescence is not only a time of physical, intellectual, and emotional change and growth but also a time when youth may examine the spiritual inheritance in which they have been imbedded and decide what in this inheritance they want to claim for themselves, what they want to question, and what they want to reject.

Perhaps adolescence is a time when parents, pastors, educators, and teachers of adolescents can step back and ask reflective questions such as:

- Who is the God these youth have encountered?

- In what ways has the Christian faith been represented to them?

- What biblical stories have they had a chance to hear and think about and respond to?

- What language of the faith is part of their vocabulary?

- What evidence have they seen of the church's involvement and commitment to mission and ministry in the community?

- What stories of Jesus do they know and what sense do they make of his roles as messiah, teacher, healer, revolutionary, or savior?

- In what ways have they experienced the sustaining presence of God's spirit in their life, the life of their family, and the church?

- When have they received pastoral care?

- When have they had opportunities to serve others?

- How have their gifts been used in the life and worship of the congregation?

- How has the Christian faith been represented to them by the ministers and leaders of the congregation?

If making a home for faith has been a value in the life of the family, then adolescence can be a time of raising the windows a bit for more air and opening the blinds to let in the light of the sun by day and the moon by night. Adolescence is a season of life when doors can be opened to new questions, experiences of faith and life, bringing to voice the certainties, questions, and doubts that are both timeless and universal.

A Faithful Formation

Craig Dykstra writes:

> A major task for adolescents is to find, among the available alternatives, a way of life that they can make their own. The search for such a way is made partly through experimentation. And the test by which adolescents finally make enduring choices is whether or not one (or more) of the patterns helps them make sense of themselves and the world. Of course, enduring choices often are not made during adolescence but only later.[6]

In thinking about the spiritual lives of adolescents, six sources are helpful. James Fowler and John Westerhoff focus on faith from a developmental perspective. Robert Kegan, Walter Brueggemann, and James Marcia speak from developmental, biblical, and counseling perspectives about transitions in life. And the work of the Search Institute contributes learnings from their research on adolescents and marks of faith maturity. Considering them individually as well as collectively provides a perspective on the ways this particular age group grows in faith.

James Fowler's research and writing in the area of faith formation and development has, I believe, added an important dimension to our understanding of human growth. Fowler has described elementary aged children as mythic-literal, "the awakening of the capacity for narrative. The child is ready not only to hear and repeat stories, but to tell stories and to conserve meanings in and through narratives."[7] This capacity for understanding faith through storytelling is illustrated in most church school curriculum that has biblical stories as the major focus with elementary school age children.

Adolescence represents a transition to a stage Fowler describes as synthetic-conventional. Marked by a growing sense of their own identity, adolescents are able to see themselves as others see them. In Fowler's terms, they are being "mirrored in new ways. The mirroring enables the person of selfhood to form a set of beliefs, values, and attitudes that can sustain the forming sense of identity as s/he takes a place in a community of con-forming others."[8] The question for the adolescent becomes, what do I believe? What beliefs are important to me and in what ways do my beliefs relate to the faith community of which I am part.

Building on the work of Fowler, educator John Westerhoff has suggested that there are four faith styles. Young children experience faith through the loving and caring hands of people in the church. Elementary age children grow in faith through a style Westerhoff describes as affiliative. They learn about faith as they come to know what it means to belong to a faith community, as they hear and read biblical stories and as they watch their congregation live out its faith in the community. For adolescents, faith is marked by a style of searching. Expressions of doubt or critical thinking, seeking knowledge or experiences of other faith traditions are part of the adolescent journey for identity and self-expression. For Westerhoff, an owned faith describes place of adults whose beliefs ground their thinking and their actions in the world.[9]

Just as children are formed with the values of their parents, they are also formed in their experiences of the Christian life through their congregational participation. In one community the lodging of homeless people during the winter months is shared by a variety of congregations who each take one night a week hosting shelter guests for dinner, a bed, and breakfast.

In one of these sponsoring congregations, shelter guests join church members for a Wednesday night meal. Individuals and families volunteer to help with setup, laundry, and administration. Each week in the worship bulletin, the supplies needed for Room in the Inn are listed with a particular request for each month: socks, travel-size toothpaste, lip balm, lotion, and a basket is available outside the sanctuary for contributions.

A teenager who goes with his family to Wednesday night fellowship remembers sharing a meal with one of the guests who talked about his love of art and drawing. In recalling this story, the teenager tells about seeing the guest's drawing pencils and realizing how small they had become. He said, "We went to the resource room and found a new set of art pencils for him to take with him when he left."

While searching to name and claim a faith and belief that is their own, adolescents continue to be formed in faith through experiences of acting in faith offered by their church. Churches that actively involve themselves in issues of justice for homeless, persons facing the death penalty, health care, persons with mental and emotional or physical disabilities provide experiential opportunities for adolescents to connect the words and teachings of Jesus with the realities of living in our world today.

Robert Kegan is an educator whose thinking was considered in Chapter 1 in relation to issues of human development and growth. A part of his theory that relates to growing in faith is his concept of the role that the culture plays in human development. He has said that humans live within a culture of embeddedness. Such a culture has three functions: confrontation, contradiction, and continuity, or holding on, letting go, and remaining in place.[10]

While Kegan speaks from the stance of a developmental educator, Walter Brueggemann looks at life through the lens of a Hebrew Bible scholar. His work with the book of Psalms provides a window on the heart and soul of the psalmists and their struggles with belief and faith. Brueggemann has taught us about the power of the psalms of lament, which comprise the largest category of kinds of psalms. Lament psalms typically illustrate three situations in the life of the psalmist, that of being securely oriented, disoriented, and then reoriented.[11]

Both Kegan and Brueggemann are speaking about change and transitions in life. Consider their three steps in relation to adolescents and faith. Youth who are embedded with the faith tradition of their family grow up with the experiences of being part of a congregation. They grow up learning the stories of the Bible. As their cognitive abilities develop and they struggle with questions of faith, belief, questions about God's activity with humankind, there is a time of disorientation (Bruggemann) or contradiction (Kegan).

Adolescents are growing into adult capacities both to raise essential questions and to move deeply into the mysteries of God. Their questions lead them to new places of being reoriented (Bruggemann) to a new place in relation to God, until the next time of disorientation.

We teach children to pray by praying for them, praying with them, teaching them to form their own prayers. We also tell them that God hears their prayers. We hope we also teach them that God doesn't always answer prayers in ways that we expect. A teenager wonders about the existence of God. When asking her to say more, it becomes clearer that her questions about the existence of God are tied up with her concern for the health of her sick grandmother. She has prayed for healing for her grandmother, but the results she has hoped for are not readily apparent. This young woman is confronted with what she has been taught and is living with the realities of the contradictions she is experiencing.

As she reflects on who God is and the practice of prayer, other theological issues emerge: What good is prayer? Does God always answer prayers? What if I don't see immediate results? In struggling with such questions, she joins all the people of faith who have gone before her, like the psalmist who asks of God, "Hear, O Lord, when I cry aloud, be gracious to me and answer me! . . . Your face, Lord, do I seek. Do not hide your face from me" (Ps. 27:7–9).

In discussing the issue of identity formation in adolescence, psychologist James Marcia identified late adolescence (ages eighteen to twenty-one) as a time of crisis and commitment. His research identified these categories appropriate for this specific age group within adolescence:

> Achievement—These are young people who have a clear sense of identity and have found a sense of commitment in their lives.
>
> Moratorium—These adolescents are living in crisis, attempting to resolve it by examining a variety of life options.
>
> Foreclosure—The beliefs and commitments of this adolescent (often influenced by their parents) are locked in, not open to question or examination.
>
> Diffusion—Personal commitments are not yet identified or even being sought by this adolescent.[12]

Consider these categories from a different angle of vision, one of faith, and adolescents themselves ages twelve to eighteen. Although used by Marcia to describe issues of identity formation, I think they also describe adolescents in their movement to name and claim a faith that is their own. Within the life span of a teenager, middle school, junior high and high school, any or all of those categories can be observed. Some adolescents will display one or several of them. Some will not experience these until they are young adults.

Parents, teachers, and pastors of youth are in a unique place to listen to their questions, their "theological epiphanies," as Kathleen Norris would describe them. Within a confirmation class of younger and middle-age adolescents, it is possible to see all four viewpoints represented. One teenager, because of a personal crisis in her life of faith, raises questions about the very existence of God. Another has identified himself as an agnostic (moratorium). These two young people are seeking a space for raising their own questions about God and their own beliefs.

Another teenager has inherited the belief commitments of her or his parents and adopted them as his or her own. When asked to express their own opinion or to ask their own question, often such youth are unable to step outside of the faith identity of their parents and family to express their own voice of faith. Others are quite articulate and are able to express the faith commitments they have inherited. The question for faith identity here would be, "Has the opportunity for individual naming and claiming of faith been foreclosed?"

For some adolescents, issues of faith and life are "not on their screen," so to speak. Thinking about God as Creator, Redeemer, and Spirit, God's self-revelation through scripture and the life of the Christian in the world are not important at this time in their life. For other adolescents, faith and being part of a congregation are established as an important commitment in their life. For some adolescents, talking about issues of faith is not as formative for them as is participating with their family in the life and mission of a congregation.

In 1990, the Search Institute reported the results of their study about faith and marks of faith maturity. They based their definition of an integrated faith on Matthew 22:34–39, which is Jesus' answer to the question of the disciples, "What is the greatest commandment?" which was "Love the Lord your God with all your heart, with all your soul and with all your might. And the second is like it, you shall love your neighbor as yourself." The marks of faith that they believe help to define a Christian are these: trusting and believing, seeking spiritual growth, integrating faith and life, holding life-affirming values, experiencing the fruits of faith, nurturing faith in community, advocating social change, and acting and serving.[13] These marks of faith should not be new ideas because they are articulated in mission or membership statements of Protestant denominations. These marks of faith are explicit in articles in church newsletters and announcements in worship bulletins. They are visible in the lives of Christians who are active in the life of a congregation.

This section on faithful formation began with a quote by Craig Dykstra that suggests that a task of adolescent spiritual development is making sense out of a variety of choices by beginning to claim and name a belief system that is their own. He goes on to affirm what many theological educators believe, that this activity of searching and claiming faith continues through young adulthood and even later.

In the first chapter, Kegan's image for adolescent development of the bridge anchored firmly on each end with challenge and support applies with spiritual development as well. Families and congregations that work to help adolescents ask the hard questions about the Bible, faith, and life are supporting them in their search to make a life of faith their own. The last sections of this chapter will address some practical ways of challenging and supporting a teenager's growth in faith.

Faithful Practices

Recent literature in the religious genre has been making use of the term religious practices to describe the things we do on a daily basis that have the potential for deepening our life of the Christian faith, of connecting us to the mysteries of God and indeed the practical ways we live our lives in relation to the Holy One who is both transcendent and immanent. Consider these additional ways that religious practices have been defined.

Robert Wuthnow describes a practice as a "cluster of activities that is pursued deliberately. It takes time and energy and it requires one's attention, meaning that the pursuit of any particular practice is accomplished only at the sacrifice of other possible activities." Wuthnow believes that children "grow up religious" through "specific, deliberate religious activities that are firmly intertwined with the daily habits of family routines, of eating and sleeping, of having conversations, of adorning the spaces in which people live, of celebrating the holidays, and of being part of a community. . . . . Embedded practices are influential in religious development because they spin out webs of significance that richly connect people with the world around them."[14]

Dorothy Bass has said that practices are defined as "those shared activities that address fundamental needs and that, woven together, form a way of life. Reflecting on practices as they have been shaped in the context of Christian faith leads us to encounter the possibility of a faithful way of life, one that is both attuned to present-day needs and taught by ancient wisdom."[15]

In identifying fourteen practices significant for Christians, Craig Dykstra has said that they "place people in touch with God's redemptive activity, that put us where life in Christ may be made known, recognized, experienced, and participated in. They [practices] are means of grace, the human places in which and through which God's people come to faith and grow to maturity in the life of faith."[16]

Spiritual disciplines have often been associated with the lives of cloistered men and women who live in Christian communities. Disciplines of faith, such as prayer and worship, mark the hours of the day between for the community gathered together and for the life of the individual. From the outside, we look on such people of faith as deeply spiritual, a place that we can never attain.

I am intrigued by the notion of practices in the ongoing conversations about spirituality. To speak of spirituality in terms of a "practice" rather than a "discipline" moves it into the realm of the daily and the possible, something I want to do rather than the "oughtness" of a discipline. Dykstra has identified these fourteen practices that he believes are significant for Christians:

1. Worshiping God together

2. Telling the Christian story to one another

3. Interpreting together the Scriptures and the history of the church's experience

4. Praying together and by ourselves

5. Confessing our sin to one another, and forgiving and becoming reconciled

6. Tolerating one another's failures and encouraging one another

7. Carrying out faithful acts of service and witness together

8. Giving of what one has and receiving gifts from others

9. Suffering with and for one another

10. Providing hospitality and care—to those we know, to strangers, to enemies

11. Listening and talking with others

12. Struggling to understand the context of life

13. Criticizing and resisting the powers of evil that destroy human beings, corrode human community, and injure God's creation

14. Working together to maintain and create social structures that sustain life in accordance with God's will.[17]

As you read this list, consider your response to these questions:

Which of these practices were part of your childhood?

What place do you make for these practices in your life of faith now?

How important are these practices in the life of your family, the life of your teenager?

Did any practice on this list surprise you? Is there a spiritual practice that you would add?

In reading this list, I am struck by its ordinariness, how the activities fit into our daily way of living. Walking outside our home, you meet a neighbor, have a conversation, and catch up on their life. Over coffee, in backyards, or talking on the back steps of your apartment building, you listen to stories of loss and grief, joys and concerns. Teenagers suffer with friends who are in physical or emotional pain. At family meals, when sharing about each other's day and the events in the world, children grow up learning how to understand the context of life and how we are called to live it as Christians.

Thinking of spirituality in terms of these practices means we acknowledge the mystery of God in the daily activities in which we are engaged. It means we name them as religious. We put language and action together. Dykstra suggests that we hunger for religious language and asks, "Could it be that we do not know our faith's language because we simply do not live the form of life out of which such language grows? Perhaps our form of life is, in reality, so fully governed by another language that religious language is simply quaint and irrelevant."[18]

Nurturing a Growing Faith

By the time a child reaches adolescence, we hope seeds of faith have been planted and carefully tended in her or his life. Participation in the life and ministry of a congregation and "growing up religious" at home have provided an important beginning for Christian formation. Three questions are essential in considering the concept of a faith that grows:

1. Adolescents who have grown up in a faithful congregation know and have experienced the language of faith and worship and the biblical story. In what ways do we continue to nurture their spiritual selves? How do we as parents, pastors, and teachers of youth encourage and support their continuing growth in the life of the Christian faith?

2. How do our programs of Christian education and our practices of worship invite or prevent teenagers from being interested in being active participants and leaders?

3. Why do some parents require their teenager's participation in confirmation and why does confirmation, for some youth, become the point of their graduation from participation in the life, work, and mission of a congregation?

I think Dykstra is correct when he says that:

Religious language, is at its heart, the language of poetry and story. . . . The care and education of youth (as well as the well-being of our society) demands the recovery of lively, vital, usable religious language. . . . This is a very difficult task. It involves the recovery of language that is clear enough to be comprehended by young people, rich enough to be meaningful, concrete enough to relate to the world as it is, and critical enough to keep open the dynamics of inquiry and continuing conversation. Moreover, it involves providing help in—teaching of, even—the art of interpretation.[19]

Notice the expectations Dykstra believes are required in recovering religious language with youth—clear, rich, concrete, and critical. They can become guidelines for mentoring an adolescent in faith. We nurture the spiritual selves of teenagers in clear and rich ways by continuing to involve them in the life of a faithful congregation, in opportunities for church school, worship, and times of community—church breakfasts, Wednesday evening fellowship, church retreats.

We nurture their spiritual selves in concrete and critical ways when we engage with them in service and mission, fixing meals for homeless guests, working together on projects in and around the church, going on CROP walks, visiting church members in retirement or nursing care facilities, taking stands for and witnessing against structures in our society that work against sustaining human life.

One reality of adolescent development is the visible change in their appearance. Parents of teenagers get used to hearing comments about their teenager from other adults in the congregation, "He's so tall, I can't believe how fast he is growing," or, "It seems like yesterday she was just a child, and now she's a young woman." What about the connection between their development and the ways that teenagers participate and share their time, talents, gifts, and/or abilities within a congregation? The second question on page 43 addresses this issue in terms of hospitality. They are growing in both confidence and ability in areas of particular interest, such as art, music, drama, dance, science and technology, or sports.

Teenagers, like adults, grow competent in their abilities to lead in worship by serving as liturgists, liturgical dancers, or musicians. One church had a set of bells and invited children or teenagers to come with a parent and play in the bell choir. Some of the people best able to work with churches on maintaining their Web sites are teenagers who refer to themselves as "computer geeks."

We notice the physical changes that tell us they are no longer children. Do we notice the accompanying growth in confidence in their areas of special interest? When we welcome the use of their gifts, we are welcoming their leadership in ways that are clear, rich, and concrete, and in so doing, we help them grow in their recovery of religious language. In recognizing their growing talents and abilities, we also invite their questions, their critical reflections on faith and life, church, and practices of faith.

When a congregation welcomes the participation and leadership of its youth, it is making a commitment to continue to live out its baptismal promises. The waters of baptism that marked a child for a life of faith also mark the changes a congregation must face in welcoming new ones to their community. In what ways is the welcome mat for the clear, rich, concrete, and critical faith language of adolescents made evident at the doors of your church?

I began the last section of this chapter with three questions essential for nurturing the growing life of faith of adolescents. The first question focuses on adolescents and the second one is concerned with congregations. The third one addresses the other partner in adolescents growing in the life of faith, parents. I am concerned about parents who believe confirmation is a graduation exercise. I am concerned about parents whose participation in the life of a congregation has a term limit—"I'll participate as long as my children do," or, "I want my children to grow up in the church." Implicit behind these statements is that the church can give children something, that is, belief or faith, which their parents either don't want, don't need, or believe can best be done by professionals.

If adolescents are to continue their growth in their knowledge and experience of the Christian faith, the most important mentors will continue to be their parents, people who struggle with them through affirmations of faith, with doubts and questions, and with the realities of connecting the holy and the ordinary. Parents are in an essential location to help youth recover religious language that is clear, rich, concrete, and critical. Parents can be bridges of challenge and support for a teenager's growth in the life of faith; or they can be ones whose lack of any involvement or support in the development of their teenager's spiritual self will be an obstacle to overcome.

The day in and day out living with a teenager provides countless opportunities for helping them interpret what they see, what they feel, what they have experienced in light of the reality of God who says, "Do not fear, for I have redeemed you; I have called you by name, you are mine. When you pass through the waters, I will be with you; and through the rivers, they shall not overwhelm you; when you walk through fire you shall not be burned, and the flame shall not consume you. For I am the Lord your God, the Holy One of Israel, your Savior" (Is. 43:1–3).

A Psalm of Trust and Lament—Psalm 27

Read through Psalm 27 and notice what David, the author, is saying. Look first at verses 1–6. Biblical scholars say this psalm represents a combination of two kinds of psalms. Verses 1–6 are representative of a type of psalm that expresses trust or confidence in God.

Read verses 7–14. They represent a kind of psalm called an individual lament, which follows a simple form: an address to God, a complaint, a confession of trust in God, the expression of a request or petition to God, words of assurance. The psalm concludes with words of praise.[20]

Think about this interesting combination in one psalm of words of trust and confidence in God and words of lament that are "an appeal to God's compassion to intervene and change a desperate situation."[21] How would you articulate a psalm of lament? Spend some moments working with the form of a lament. How would you express your sense of trust and confidence in God?

Poet Ann Weems expressed petition and confidence in God in her lament psalm in this way:

Find me, O caring God,

Before night falls,

Because I have no light.

Take up your lantern

and look for me

before I die of fright.

I will nestle in the hope

of your coming.

You will find me

and carry me

to the path

that leads home.

I will no longer fear,

or you, O God,

you are my home![22]

3

Good-Enough Parents

Scanning the shelves at your favorite bookstore for books on raising teenagers can be both comforting and frightening. You may come across Michael J. Bradley's book, *Yes, Your Teen Is Crazy! Loving Your Kid without Losing Your Mind*, and read "contemporary parenting is a complex set of learned skills, many of which seem counterintuitive to us. . . . Successfully parenting an adolescent in today's world requires levels of skill, endurance, and strength that make piloting an aircraft pale in comparison."[1]

You thought you were doing okay as a parent, and you discover the chapter "Your Adolescent's World: Sex, Drugs, and Rock 'n Roll Like You Never Saw," in which he writes that we have "created a world dripping with sex, drugs, and violence and plunked our temporarily insane children in the middle of it. Our wonderful economy has also provided unprecedented quick-path avenues of easy access to these things. It is an adolescent world different from the one you recall."[2] Reading this, you realize the seat belt for parents moving through adolescence might not be adequate.

You move on to mysteries, a great escape for book lovers. You are reading one of the best mystery writers, Carolyn Heilbrun, writing as Amanda Cross, and come across this quote from one of her characters: "Is it as awful as they say, living with teenagers?" "Yes and no," she said. "Yes, because they have to break away and act as though their parents couldn't and didn't have the right slant on anything." No, because we had so frantically girded our loins in anticipation of nameless horrors that the actual experience seems mild by comparison—at least for the present."[3] You breathe in and out again and realize that living with an adolescent requires a lot of deep breaths, a lot of humble admissions of, "No, I probably did make a mistake, I was wrong," and some proud affirmations of "Yes, I did know what I was doing in saying no. I'm the parent here. It's my job."

You return home from this bookstore experience and turn to your page-a-day calendar and find this quote from James Baldwin, "Children have never been very good at listening to their elders, but they have never failed to imitate them." And you sit with the memories of all the times and places with your teenager and wonder what they have learned from their experiences with you as their parent.

Last year a small item made the news in the Nashville paper. It seems that a local country music star was dining in what the papers called a "family restaurant." At another table, a family was celebrating their daughter's sixteenth birthday party with a meal and a male stripper invited by the daughter's father for entertainment. The music star complained to the parents and to the management of the restaurant regarding the appropriateness of that kind of entertainment being allowed in a place of business where children, teenagers, and family were dining. The newspaper recorded the father's response, which basically was, "It's our party, our business, she shouldn't have intervened."

It seems like a distant time when the major disagreements between parents and their teenage children focused on the length of hair on their head, the length of skirts they wore, or sex outside of marriage. Add to that: body piercing; body tattoos; drugs that destroy minds, bodies, and lives; guns; sexual and domestic violence that continues to occur in great numbers in homes, schools, with kids on dates, and on the World Wide Web; depression and other emotional illnesses; neighborhoods and schools that are not safe places.

I wonder if Bradley is right that parenting today requires a "complex set of learned skills" or is it more about parenting with open eyes, ears, hands, and heart. In what ways is the parenting of a two-year-old different from parenting a fourteen-year-old? Parents protect young children from things that may hurt them in the home—electrical outlets, cabinets with toxic cleaning supplies. Meals are prepared that are balanced and healthy. Young children begin to hear the word "no" a lot, which warns them of dangers—"No, don't touch, it's hot." "No, we don't run into the street. We always hold hands to cross." We praise young children for the things they learn to do on their own and tell them, "Good job," or, "You're getting so big, look what you've learned to do."

We dress them and help them learn about colors and clothes that match, and why baths are important. We invite friends over for play dates to enable a child's developing social skills and making friends. Family rituals of mealtimes and blessings, helping others, going to church, bedtime stories and prayers, and visiting family form children in values that are embedded experientially in their lives. The quote from author James Baldwin is realized.

I think that parenting an adolescent today requires remembering that the ways we parented a two- or three-year-old still apply. We are still concerned about the same things. We are dealing with many of the same issues but with less control over the life of the teenager. They have seen the choices we have made as their parents and have been formed in this culture of family values. The role of parents shifts a bit to helping them understand the choices with which they are presented and how to make good choices and decisions that ultimately affect their behavior and thus their life. William Myers has described adolescence as a journey,

> perhaps a ten-year span, from eleven or twelve to the early twenties. From what to what? A doctor might say "from not being able to produce babies to being able to produce and care for children"; a sociologist might say " the period in which the individual passes from family life into cultural existence; a therapist might say "from being a once powerless and morally submissive child into being a care-giver and lawyer for the next generation"; a theologian might say "from inheriting a second-hand faith into owning a faith as one's own."[4]

And a parent might say from being someone who was totally dependent on me to becoming a person able to make his or her own choices and decisions, one who needs a parent not to tell them what to do but to help them consider the options faced in decision making.

This chapter offers a brief look at what educators are saying about parents, teenagers, and family life. It also offers some educational designs for use with parents in short-term learning opportunities in the church. One way this chapter could be helpful is in assessing the kinds of ministry offered by the church in support of parents of teenagers.

Hearing the Voices of Adolescents

When you close your eyes and hear the voice of a teenager you know, what do you hear? When you watch a teenager interact with peers, what do you see? Hear the voices of some adolescents. As you read this quotes, where do you see similarities with and differences from the adolescents you know and love?

I know I'm young and I don't expect to be treated like an adult, but I would like to be treated like a human being. If grown-ups would be more candid with young people, it wouldn't distress them, it would help them sort things out and have hope for the future. . . . My mom and I can talk about anything and everything together. . . . By the teen years it's too late to try and start up a tight relationship with your kid. When my anorexia started taking over at puberty, I doubt my mom would have even had a chance of helping me get well if I didn't already know that I could count on her to be on my side.[5]

I'm Chinese—both my parents are from China. I'm first generation, but my parents came over when they were in their early teens. They're still traditional, but they're kind of Americanized. . . . I started hanging out with more colored people, more racially diverse people. I have Latin, black, Asian friends . . . everything, I guess. I didn't know why I changed, why I had this decline of grades. I don't know if it was just the high school experience, or I wasn't into school. This school is not really diverse, the way I see it- and my parents would be all, 'Why don't you hang out with more Asian people?' and nah-nah-nah; and I'm all, "Well, there aren't any Asian people."[6]

My dad started a masonry company forty-five years ago. . . . I've been working with him since I was fifteen. I never really accelerated academically in school and was always a lot more interested in working with my dad than going to class or doing my homework. I know I've got a lot of common sense. I'm far from stupid, but I just can't stand sitting in class. As soon as I turned sixteen, I started working for my dad full time. . . . My dad is teaching me everything he knows. . . . Working together has definitely made us closer.[7]

I moved to Chicago because I had problems with my mother for a while—a lot of problems— so she sent me to my father. I don't really remember too much about all the frustrations and anger I had, but my mother just couldn't deal with me any- more—I was getting too violent. I had friends here and there, just moving around from one place to another. I didn't go to school too much at that time. I hated homework; I would make up stories to say why I didn't do it. I used to be little liar, some- times—I just liked storytelling. . . . I didn't really know my father, because he was always working. He tried. . . . We'd go out together and stuff like that—but we never got a chance to see him too much. When I came here, me and my father, we used to fight a lot. We got closer, but it took a lot of struggle, a lot of work. I love him a lot, too; I'm proud of a lot of things he's accomplished. But at the time I didn't care too much about what happened to him.[8]

Teenagers care more about what their friends think and say than what their parents want. Peer pressure is everything and that's why it's important not to hang around with the wrong crowd. I chose an older crowd to hang with because I wanted to feel grown. Now my childhood is gone and I regret it. I learned a lot but it cost a lot.[9]

Present in these voices are themes of relationship with parents and peers, the challenges of living in a multicultural world, and vocational hopes and realities. Michael Riera is an educator who has worked with many teenagers over the years. He describes the changes faced in adoles- cence in terms of "horizons of meanings": physical and cognitive; social; friendship; personal identity; and family and life events. "These un- avoidable changes, taken together, serve as the necessary context for making sense of teenage behaviors and attitudes."[10]

Also present in these voices are expressions of love, hope, regret, and affirmation for parents. Now return to the voices of teenagers you know. What would they say about you, your role as a parent or familial pres- ence in their life?

Thinking about Adolescents and Parents

Six educators have reflected on the nature of family. David Elkind provides a historical and cultural analysis of family. In the modern era, the nuclear family of a married couple with children, and often a mother who stayed at home, was lifted up as a value in the culture. "It was extolled as the ideal family form most suited to the rearing of children who would become responsible, productive citizens."[11] A post-modern world, which is marked by some as beginning mid-twentieth century, has produced what Elkind calls a permeable family: "Unlike the nuclear family that was walled off from the rest of society, the permeable family is open to any and all social influences. The permeable family includes a variety of kinship structures such as two-working-parent families, single-parent families, adoptive families, remarried families, and so on."[12] Family today can also be grandparents raising their grandchildren for their son or daughter. Family can be female or male partners raising an adopted child or a biological child of one of the partners from a previous relationship. Family is divorced parents sharing joint custody of their child or children.

Young Pai is an educator whose research into Asian adolescents offers another perspective, that of a web. He uses this image because he believes that "our young people live their lives in a very complex network of relationships. Indeed, their world consists of many different intersecting, overlapping and interacting cultural strands. . . . They must relate to the cultures of their Anglo adolescent contemporaries, their school, the larger American society, their parents, and adult Asian North American community."[13]

Based on her work as a therapist with teenagers and their parents, Mary Pipher has suggested that family serves as a shelter for its members. She borrows a Sioux word, *tiospaye*, which means "the people with whom one lives" to describe an extended family of relatives and friends. Pipher believes that *tiospaye*

> offers children a corrective factor for problems in their nuclear families. If parents are difficult, there are other adults around to soften and diffuse the situation. . . . What tiospaye offers and what biological family offers is a place that all members can belong to regardless of merit. Everyone is included regardless of health, likeability or prestige. . . . Many people do not have

access to either a supportive biological family or a tiospaye. They make do with a "formed family." Others simply prefer a community of friends to their biological families.[14]

Ron Taffel distinguishes between the first family with whom the teenager is related and the second family of her or his peers, the people with whom they don't have to explain themselves, a place where they are at home, comfortable. "When you enter their world, get involved with something they're interested in, kids won't automatically want to exclude you simply because you're an adult. Today's teen is surprisingly receptive to spending comfort time with adults—as long as the grownup doesn't try to be someone he or she is not."[15] Essential for parents, Taffel believes, is having an "empathic envelope" that "balances empathy and expectations, so that kids feel held by the first family at home. . . . The empathic envelope is made up of your values, your expectations, and your ways of spending time with your children. Family life occurs on the edges of the envelope, especially with teens who are constantly pushing, haggling, and renegotiating its borders."[16]

Taffel believes it is important for parents to make room for "comfort time"—when they pay attention to what their kids watch, listen to, and are interested in: "Teenagers know that they also can have in their first family the sense of ease and support they typically get from their second family."[17]

Wade Rowatt speaks of the role of adults with teenagers in terms of shepherding:

> We cannot protect adolescents from the revolution within their bodies and brains, but we can be a safe place for testing whatever emerges. . . . Accepting them as "works in progress" paves the way for them becoming more mature. Teens are not yet who they will be. . . . At best we shepherd the process of developing strong bodies, effective minds, and passionate souls.[18]

Rowatt borrows the image of shepherd from the Bible and identifies six dimensions of the work of a shepherd: healing and reconciling, sustaining and confronting, guiding and informing.[19] Notice how Rowatt pairs these activities of a shepherding process so that each has elements of both comfort and challenge.

Nick Stinnett and John DeFrain are two educators whose research in the 1980s focused on interviews with families about what enabled them to succeed. In evaluating their findings they came to define strong families as "places where we enter for comfort, development, and regeneration and places from which we go forth renewed and charged with power for positive living."[20] In listening to the stories from the thousands of families they interviewed, they determined that strong families were able to survive difficulties and challenges because of the members support for each other. Strong families gave evidence of enjoyment, happiness, and an environment in which members felt good about themselves and about their family.[21]

Integrating the Wisdom

The images that emerge from the research and writing of people who work with adolescents and families are clear. Pipher describes the family in terms of a shelter that offers protection and support. Pai suggests that a web is a helpful way to understand the world of adolescents as they move in and out of many relationships and experiences. Taffel's concern with the second family of friends of adolescents leads him to suggest that what parents need to provide for their teenage children is an empathic envelope that offers a balance of expectation and understanding, and Rowatt works with the biblical image of the shepherd to describe a role needed by adolescents. Stinnett and DeFrain speak of family in terms of those qualities that hold it together, make it strong.

I am always intrigued by what experts put on their lists. In thinking about adolescents and families, I came across four such lists variously described as principles, ten commandments, characteristics, and traits. One of them focuses on parents and three focus on the family. Before you look at these lists, take a few minutes and consider your own list. Use the space below for your thoughts.

When I think about being the parent of an adolescent, these are the most important things to remember:

Now locate them in the back of this book in Appendix 2, page 131. Look over the four lists and compare them with yours. Where are the similarities and the differences?

Bradley's list of commandments focus on the kind of parent an adolescent needs. His use of humor, like respecting an adolescent's self-expression even when he or she chooses green hair is, I think, a way to encourage parents to step back, get some perspective, to remember to choose which battles you choose to fight with your child who wants more decision-making control in his or her life.

When I look over these lists, there is one principle that appears on all four—communication and listening. Bradley's commandment of adding fifteen minutes to each interaction, or allowing time for extended reflection and conversation, is, he says, a way of allowing enough time to make important decisions. "The potential consequences of your reactions to your kid are so high that you must never get backed into schedule commitment corners when making tough decisions."[22]

A second principle on three of the lists is time. Pipher also speaks of time as one thing that shelters families. Time has become one of our most treasured possessions today. Adults wish for more hours in a day to get everything done. Parents want more time to fit in work, parenting, maintaining a home. The appellation "24/7" has become an accepted shorthand description for living in this culture.

The two lists on traits of healthy families mention the value of spirituality or religion. I have often thought that the two items missing from Pipher's list of things that shelter families are faith, or as Curran states it "a shared religious core," and participation in a congregation or faith community. Families with adolescents who make a priority of their time for nurturing a life of Christian faith by actively participating in a congregation are making explicit statements about what is important.

Implications for Congregational Support of Parents and Families

Congregations provide a fitting forum for listening and reflecting on the time pressures, work load, and dilemmas of families today. . . . There is a real need to provide a holding environment, a safe, dependable, predictable, trustworthy, sustaining space, which will allow open communication about the current

gender, familial, relational, marital, intergenerational, and vocational strife of everyday life."[23]

Recall recent times of prayers of the people in worship and the joys
and concerns that were expressed. Bonnie Miller McLemore has suggested there are not only acceptable things that can be mentioned but
also many authentic issues that are never mentioned: alcohol and drug
addiction, domestic violence, infertility, abortion, family conflicts, job
loss. Janet Fishburn speaks of this reality in terms of a "conspiracy of
silence" in congregations that do not have a model of ministry that provides space and time for dealing with the real issues of what happens in
families.

Scanning the bookshelves on adolescents in your local bookstore
can be both affirming and frightening at the same time. Books on adolescents written for parents often include chapters on these issues:

> Family issues—trust, communication, privacy, divorce,
> independence

> Sexuality—dating, date rape, being gay, romance, breakup,
> pregnancy, abortion, parenthood

> Peer and academic pressures—making decisions, learning
> disabilities, after high school what?

> Youth violence—date rape, weapons at home and in schools;
> physical violence within the family

> Depression and suicide

> Substance and physical abuse—drinking and driving, drugs,
> eating disorders

When you consider this list of issues, one reaction could be, "At least
I'm only having to deal with a few of these and they really aren't life-
threatening." Another response could be, "Oh no, am I naïve to think I
won't have to deal with some of the harder things on this list?" And
finally, the parent who has already experienced some of the more dis-
turbing of these realities in the life of their teenager, lives in fear with
what will happen next and the "conspiracy of silence" that surrounds
their family as they go through it alone.

What if the church became a place of support and challenge for parents of adolescents? What if the church became a place where parents felt safe and free to share their own struggles with faith and life with their teenager? As Janet Fishburn has said, "When important parts of life are not subject to theological reflection, people are not able to believe that God's grace really is at work there."[24] Parents of teenagers are certainly ones who need to remember their calling to tell and live the story of God to their children "so that they should set their hope in God, and not forget the works of God" (Ps. 78:7).

An Educational Model for Ministry with Parents of Teenagers

Models for pastoral and educational ministry with youth and families vary according to the size and priorities. Some churches are large enough to have a minister for youth and young adults on their staff. Other churches hire a young adult to work as a youth director. Many congregations rely on and nurture the development and support of church members to work with youth in teaching, youth ministry programs, and mission. Such models for youth ministry rightly focus on programs, mission, and pastoral care with youth themselves. Models for education and ministry with parents of teenagers is a much lower priority for congregations and in some cases is nonexistent.

Described below are some educational designs for use with parents of teenagers. Any of these could fit into a model for ministry with parents. Some of the designs could be offered once a year, some could be offered more infrequently or as needed. A church committee with the responsibility for nurture or education could look over these designs and make decisions about implementation.

As you look over this educational model of ministry with parents, reflect on these questions:

1. Who are the families with teenagers in your congregation: families with two parents, families with single parents, grandparents or other family members who may be helping to raise a teenager, divorced parents sharing custody of their child?

2. When are the best times to get parents together? Some churches have mid-week gathering times like Wednesday night, which

might work. What about a time for parents when youth are at church on Sunday evening? Adult education times during church school are another option.

3. Which of these ideas are already in place in your congregation?

4. Which ideas are new, ones you might want to consider trying?

5. What other ideas for ministry with and support of parents of teenagers are generated from this list?

Opportunities for Connecting and Discussion

Making Room for Family and Faith

In her book *Family: The Shelter of Us All*, Mary Pipher describes the six things she believes shelter families: time, places, interests, celebrations, connecting rituals, and stories and metaphors. I believe two other things shelter families—faith and participation in the life and ministry of a congregation.

> **Purpose:** To reflect on the ways we make room for family time as children move from childhood to adolescence. To consider the role that rituals of faith have in the life of a family.

> **Time Frame:** This educational design could work as either a three-to-four-hour workshop or a four-session discussion.

> **Teaching and Learning Activities:** Choose from among these suggestions to fit your learning context.

- Read and discuss selections from Pipher, *Family: The Shelter of Us All*: Chapter 11, "Protecting Families—Houses without Walls," and Chapter 12, "Connecting Families—Creating a Tiospaye."

- "The Good, the Bad, and the Ugly"—Involve parents in reflecting on the realities of their family life with a teenager.

- Discuss these questions:

1. What are some things we've always done as a family together that we continue now that our children are older?

2. Are there things you do as a family now that are different from when your children were small?

3. In what ways has your participation as a family in a church changed as children have grown to be teenagers?

Help, I'm the Parent of a Teenager!

This would be a good workshop or adult education opportunity for parents of children just moving into adolescence, kids who are in fourth or fifth grade making the transition from elementary school to middle school. The pastor, an educator and parent, or parents of older adolescents or young adults could share leadership for this workshop or session.

> **Purpose:** To give parents the chance: to recall what they remember about adolescent development from their own experience; to discuss challenges and opportunities of being an adolescent in today's culture; to raise issues with which they are most concerned in relation to their teenager; to share resources.
>
> **Time Frame:** Like others described here, this activity could be offered as a three-to-four hour workshop on an evening or a weekend or as three-to-four separate sessions that fit into an existing frame for adult education.
>
> **Teaching and Learning Activities:**

- "Back to the Future"—Discuss with the participants their own memories of being a teenager. Have magazines, newspapers, paper, crayons, and markers. Invite the adults first to reflect individually with collage, words, or pictures that capture their adolescent experiences.

- Invite a middle-school teacher or administrator to talk with the group about things parents can do to support their emerging teenager.

- "You Know You Have a Teenager When"—Have a panel discussion with the group on this topic. Leadership for the panel could include any or all of the following: middle-school teacher or administrator; pastor, priest, or rabbi; counselor, therapist, or psychologist; someone who teaches or works with youth in areas of art or sports; a college student or young adult; a parent who has college-age children.

- "Changes"—One teacher could be prepared to lead the group in a discussion of these issues for which Chapters 1 and 2 of this book are a resource: Changes in my child that I am beginning to observe and changes I expect in my child— emotional, physical, social, intellectual, and faith. View a video together about adolescence. See Chapter 6 for suggestions.

Friday, Saturday, or Sunday Family Nights

This could be a fun, brainstorming time for sharing ideas of things families with teenagers can continue to do together. The concept is that some families have one night a week or month that is designated as "Family Night," a time when all the family members make the commitment to be together for an evening. Some families who do this rotate among different things, such as game night (Monopoly, Scrabble, and so on); dinner and a movie; going bowling, skating, or hiking; going to something together such as a sports event, a play, music performance, or an art exhibit. Offering an opportunity like this at the church, several times a year, is a great way to support single-parent families.

> **Purpose:** To discover the wealth of ideas present in the group for things families with teenagers can go to together.

> **Time Frame:** This could easily be done in one hour. This session would also work well as an intergenerational event— youth and adults together.

Teaching and Learning Activities:

- Have index cards available. Explain the concept of a family night and ask them to write on index cards some ideas for things families with teenagers can do together. These could be things they do now or things they would like to do.

- Collect all the index cards and pass them out, asking people to read what's there.

- Introduce the concept of the liturgical calendar or seasons of the church year.

- Invite the participants to discuss what they have done at home to celebrate the seasons of the church year.

Six-week class for parents of younger adolescents or parents of youth who are in confirmation programs—read and discuss a current book together, or view and discuss a video series. Refer to the bibliography in Chapter 6 for suggestions. Follow this format:

Gathering—A psalm and a prayer

Exploring—A story from life, a member of the group volunteers each session to bring a story about an adolescent

Connecting—Discussion of a chapter from the book you are reading or view a video

Going—Summary comments, issues of faith and life raised here, focus for next session

Survival Skills for Parents and Teenagers

The transition of a child to a teenager seems to happen both slowly and yet very quickly. All of a sudden, pants are too short as are tempers. Doors to your child's bedroom are usually closed now. How do parents and teenagers survive all the changes?

Purpose: This session is designed to give parents an opportunity to consider how the changes that their child is going through impacts them and their family.

Time Frame: This could be a one time only or a monthlong learning opportunity.

I have often thought it would be interesting to offer sessions for parents of youth in confirmation education. This might be a good topic to offer at the beginning of the church school year or whenever confirmation education begins.

Teaching and Learning Activities: Choose from among these suggestions.

- Read and discuss Chapters 1 and 2 from this book. Use the quotes at the beginning of this chapter as a way to begin a discussion about the challenges and opportunities of living with a teenager.

- Look at the quote from William Myers on page 49 of this chapter. In describing the adolescent journey, he gives examples of how this would be viewed from the perspective of a doctor, a sociologist, a therapist, and a theologian. Continue with his analogy. How would a teacher describe this journey—from what to what? How do you as a parent describe this journey—from what to what?

- Think about your family and how you work together.

- Read and discuss Michael Riera's, *Uncommon Sense for Parents with Teenagers.* These chapters would be excellent for group discussion: Chapter 1—"The Parent-Adolescent Relationship"; Chapter 2—"The Adolescent World"; Chapter 3—"The High School Experience"; Chapter 5—"Limits and Structure"; Chapter 6—"Natural Consequences"; Chapter 20—Parent Mental Health." Other topical chapters may be of interest to the group, especially the ones on divorce, single parenting, remarriage, and blended families.

- Use Appendix 4 as a guide for discussion about roles of parents with teenagers. This topic would work well in a mixed group of teenagers and parents. There could be time for separate groups (youth and parents) to discuss and then mix up the groups.

- Read over the quotes in the section, "Hearing the Voices of Adolescents," page 50.

    Another session that would work well with adolescents and parents together would be to ask each one there to write a paragraph that says something about her or his own life as a teenager or a parent. These could then be shared and discussed as people are willing and able to share.

One More Thing to Put on the List

When I started to make plans for the writing of this book, my sister suggested that perhaps I might want to write it in a practical context such as her family. Perhaps, she said, if you lived with a teenager for a while, it would help you know what to write about. Living with my family has also meant being part of their church and getting to know a group of adolescents. Working with these young people, living with one, talking with parents, and observing interactions within families, I decided that the list of things to remember as a parent really does come down to four things: communication, time, humor, and self-care.

Listen—be fully present in the conversation. Teenagers are learning how to make decisions that affect their life. Listening and responding that helps them consider options and the impact of their choices is a way they learn to be responsible for their own decisions in life.

Make time—provide time and space for interactions, checking in, the extra fifteen minutes it may take to hear the words behind the silence or the emotion. Extra time enables you to see behind and beyond expressed anger or a wall of silence for the source or causes. Invite your teenager to share time and space with you.

Laugh—it's impossible to get through adolescence again (this time as a parent) without having a sense of humor—"it's a joke" is a common phrase around our house. Just when an adult is ready to blow up because of something the teenager has said, he quietly reminds her or him, "it's a joke. Get it?" And tied closely to the teenage commandment of "it's a joke" is the second, don't take it personally!

Take care of yourself—remember to take some time for yourself. Michael Riera speaks of this in terms of "parent mental health." He says that parents need to find a minimum and maximum routine each day. "Do at least a minimal amount of whatever nurtures your mental health on a daily basis."[25] What is it that helps you get through a day—exercise, meditation, prayer, reading, journaling, working in a garden, talking with a friend, even something as simple as sitting and looking out a window for five to ten minutes? Riera has said, "Remember that a large part of your role as parent is to nurture your teenager's hope. At the same time, remember to take care of your own hope too. It is what will keep you going, even on the toughest of days."[26]

In the letter to the churches of Galatia, Paul contrasts the works of the flesh with the fruits of the Spirit. "The fruit of the Spirit is love, joy, peace, patience, kindness, generosity, faithfulness, gentleness, and self-control" (Gal. 5:22–23). We love our teenagers. We may not always like them, their choices, or their attitude, but we always love them. On even a very bad day, when, like *Alexander and the Terrible, Horrible, No Good, Very Bad Day*, you would like to run away to Australia and leave your teenager behind, surely there is a moment of peace, a moment of apology and forgiveness, and shalom is present again.[27]

Patience and self-control seem to fit together for those who parent teenagers. Neither one is particularly easy but is possible. We hope our children learn to be kind and generous and surely they do when they see it modeled in the words and lives of adults they love. Faithfulness and gentleness seem also to go together when thinking about living with teenagers. Wise parents know that their children need a good balance of freedom and accountability. It truly is a gift of the spirit to know when gentleness is needed in a hard moment of being faithful to a value or a principle.

The apostle Paul goes on to say that "If we live by the Spirit, let us also be guided by the Spirit. Let us not become conceited, competing against one another, envying one another" (Gal. 5:25–26). Chapter 6 then moves into a discussion of bearing one another's burdens.

Think about your parenting role with a teenager. Think about others in your congregation and all the different configurations that are represented: single parents, grandparents or aunts or uncles raising a teenager, divorced parents, blended families, multifaith families and multicultural families. Together there is strength in this larger family of faith, strength in bearing one another's burdens and hope together that the teenagers being raised in this community will grow in the fruits of God's Spirit.

A Psalm for Parents—Psalm 78

What does it mean to be a good-enough parent? Some days, it's easier than others. In the end, it's the bigger picture, the small vignettes of life that, when looked at together, reveal a family that works together. Psalm 78 is a favorite of mine. It reminds me of my nephew's request, "tell a story about me." It is one of a special group of psalms described as "storytelling" or "historical psalms." These particular psalms are hymns that "express the shared history of the believing and worshipping community."[28] Written as hymns for use in worship, these psalms retell in a dramatic fashion, the story of God's saving action in the lives of the people of Israel. In speaking about this particular genre of psalms, Old Testament scholar Bernhard Anderson says that psalms of this kind "recite events fundamental to Israel's self-understanding as a people and essential to Israel's knowledge of who God is."[29]

The story of the acts of faithfulness and unfaithfulness of God's people were told in worship through music and drama. In the telling and hearing again of the story, in the act of remembering a shared history, the purpose of the psalm becomes one of remembering the past so as to live differently in the present and the future.

Notice where the importance is placed in the retelling of this story. We will not hide things from the children. We will tell them to the coming generation, the glorious deeds of God and the wonders God has done. We will tell them to the children "so that they should set their hope in God and not forget the works of God." (Ps. 78:7) Read the rest of the psalm and hear a familiar story. What is revealed about God's people? What is revealed about God?

In thinking about the literary form of the Psalms, Tom Long has said that "poetry stretches the ordinary uses of words, and places them into unfamiliar relationships with each other, thereby cutting fresh paths across the well-worn grooves of everyday language." Poems, he says, "make finely tuned adjustments at deep and critical places in our imaginations" because "the words penetrate directly to that place where we visualize our primary relationship with God."[30]

I love the book of Psalms. I love the form and the content—hymns that express the deepest experiences of human life. I love the Psalms because they tell the story of humankind's relationship with God. Reading the Psalms reminds me of our commitment to remember and about how we are to live in faithful response to God's acts on our behalf.

Sit with this psalm. Pray with this psalm. What is revealed to you about your primary relationship with God?

4

Confirmed and Commissioned: Connecting Faith and Life

A confirmation class was five months into its journey together. The confirmands were focusing on the Trinity and more specifically on the Redeemer. Their teacher asked them to share some adjectives they would use to describe Jesus. They responded with: Son of God, teacher, healer, and defiler, one who broke the rules. The focus for this particular session was on Jesus' work as teacher and the Beatitudes in Matthew 5 as a specific example of his teachings. Together with the help of a video, *How to Get Blessed without Sneezing*, the class discussed its understandings of the first four beatitudes.

Their teachers were helping the youth relate their understanding of the beatitudes—why Jesus selected these particular qualities as most important—with their own life experiences. As a way into a discussion of the beatitude, "Blessed are those who mourn, for they shall be comforted," one of the teachers asked the fifteen seventh and eighth graders, "Have you ever mourned the loss of something or someone? What did it feel like?" I watched the faces of the youth and immediately saw heads nod and hands rise. Two recalled the suicide of a friend at school. Another mentioned the divorce of parents and how hard it was during that time. Others shared the loss of family pets.

I was struck by the immediacy and honesty of their responses. This, of course, was not the first time these youth had encountered the role of Jesus as teacher. They had been hearing and learning stories from the Gospels during their elementary years. In this confirmation education experience, one goal was to enable the youth to express both their beliefs and their questions about the Christian faith.

For some in this class, faith in God is confidently asserted. For others, questions about the existence of God are primary. A majority of these teenagers were baptized as infants and have been raised in the life of the church. This class offers them the chance to make affirmations and raise questions as they consider what they believe and whether they are ready to publicly affirm their beliefs and be confirmed as members of their church. Some will participate without question. Others will have serious questions of faith, struggle with the decision, and may or may not decide to be confirmed at this time in their life. A few will participate because it is expected of them.

Janet Fishburn has said that Christian faith is not inherited: each generation, each individual, must learn faith anew."[1] Parents raise their children in faith, teaching them with their words and their lives. Then comes a moment when young people are given the opportunity to affirm what they believe, to name and claim faith and belief.

You may be wondering why this chapter, which focuses on confirmation and theories of learning, is included here. In some ways, it was the driving force behind this book. I keep bumping into the question raised by pastors who are most often the teachers of confirmation. They wonder why confirmation becomes graduation from church for many of our youth. "Confirmed and out the door" is the experience of many pastors. To say it more bluntly, why are baptism and confirmation certificates suitable for framing or for mounting in a family scrapbook of more value than a child or youth's ongoing participation in a community of faith? Why are congregations unable to hold on to their newest and youngest members?

Others express frustration and exasperation in teaching confirmands whose participation is not their choice but rather a parental requirement. Confirmation education programs can have within the same group youth who know the biblical stories and have many experiences of being part of a church family and youth whose experience of church is almost nonexistent. Other pastors wonder why until it's time for them to be confirmed. William Myers has stated the problem in this way:

> The current question facing the church as it once again considers what role, if any, confirmation plays, is, what is Christianity in this modern context, or indeed, who is Christ for us today? If the answer is, in part, that the church is called to be a vibrant faith community incarnating Christ's presence and welcoming

adolescents into age-appropriate shared ministry, then we cannot simply think through to such an answer. Confirmation as a hollow graduation exercise from a school is not enough.[2]

It is appropriate in a book that is written for an audience that includes parents, educators, and pastors to take time to consider this moment of confirming faith and its meaning for all of us and especially for our youth.

Faith Marker Events

Christian parents acknowledge their faith commitments when they bring their child to worship for the sacrament of infant baptism or the ritual of infant dedication. This moment marks a family and a faith community, joining them together in affirming belief in Jesus Christ as Lord and Savior, in acknowledging the presence of God's spirit moving in their life and claiming belief in God's love and presence as they journey together. Children are marked with the waters of baptism and the promises of parents to raise a child in the Christian faith, to nurture their spiritual growth as intentionally as they feed and clothe them, love and hold them. Recall words often heard at a child's baptism, "You are a child of God, sealed in the spirit in your baptism and you belong to Jesus Christ forever." There is incredible potential present in this faith marker event.

Young children grow up in the church participating with the congregation in worship, Christian education, acts of service, and mission. They learn about worship and are invited to Christ's table. In acknowledgement of their growth and developing abilities, congregations give Bibles or Bible storybooks to young elementary-age children. In so doing a church says, "Here is our story. Here is a place where we learn about God and how God wants us to live in the world." And another Bible is welcomed into a home. Here is another moment of potential for learning, sharing, reading, and inviting a child's participation.

Infant baptism or dedication and giving of Bibles to children are two public ways a congregation welcomes and affirms the faith of parents and children. In late summer or fall, when a new year of church school begins, teachers and leaders are acknowledged and dedicated in their commitments to share faith with children, youth, and adults. In worship a congregation affirms its continued commitment to tell the story, to continue to raise up generations in faith. Those same people who made promises at a child's baptism or dedication, respond as they volunteer to teach church school, work with choirs, lead youth groups, volunteer for mission trips. In acts of education, mission, worship, and ministry, we are marked in faith in very explicit and implicit ways.

In an ideal situation youth who come to confirmation are marked by these faith experiences. They bring with them all their life experiences. They have been raised by Christian parent or parents. They have read the Bible at home and know how to pray. They have had the chance to struggle with questions of faith and to see the way that faith and life are connected as they are nurtured by their parent or parents.

What Confirmation Is; What It Is Not

If you asked people in your church to define confirmation or to tell you what they think is the purpose of confirmation education, you would probably get many different responses. These responses are probably the result of both knowledge and experience and also probably vary with the perspective that comes from being a teenager, pastor, teacher, or parent. For some youth it is a requirement, something they have to do because their parents are making them do it. Remembering their own confirmation experience, some parents send their kids to confirmation with hopes and prayers they won't be bored to death. For a few youth, confirmation could be their last educational experience in the church if their parents view it as graduation. Many pastors and adults who teach confirmation genuinely look forward to this special time with youth of the church. Others consider it a requirement, "remedial Sunday school," and focus on the curriculum to the exclusion of the learners.

Is the purpose of confirmation to:

- require the memorization of creeds, biblical texts, or catechism?

- teach the basics of Christian faith and theology?

- enable youth to gain an understanding of denominational identity—including theology, polity, worship, and sacraments?

- provide space and time to ask questions, to reflect on the meaning of faith and the purpose of the church?

Consider your own definition of confirmation. What are your hopes, expectations, and goals for teaching and learning? Then look at the ones below. When you compare your definition with these, what similarities and differences do you notice? Biblical scholar, Walter Brueggemann has said this.

> Every year we "take in new members" and young people "join." But we don't reflect often on the fact that joining means belonging to and belonging with and belonging for. Our notion of church membership has gotten so institutional that it means signing a book or making a pledge. Or it has gotten so fuzzy that it means little except to satisfy the long-standing expectation of adults. In most of the ways we structure it, church membership is incidental—sort of an extra that we do like deciding where to shop or where to bank or where to go to college for awhile. . . . Church membership is joining a story, joining a vision, joining a crunch.[3]

Theological educator William Myers writes that:

> Because the rite of confirmation, in this sense, is a window into the faithfulness of congregational practice, it should be recognized, emphasized, intentionally pursued, and celebrated. This perspective affords both congregation and confirmand a rare occasion for joint growth and celebration. But this can occur only if congregations support, in the presence of older youth and adults as "living bridges"—witnesses, storytellers, spiritual guides, companions, and co-ministers—a variety of healthy, purposeful roles for adults and confirmands within the ongoing practices of the church. The faith stance that identifies the church (God knows, loves, and affirms the worth of all peoples, including adolescents) must be incarnated, or practiced in real ways.[4]

Robert Browning and Roy Reed have written extensively about the history and practice of confirmation education:

> Confirmation as blessing by God, the faith community and the family should have a relational quality which is empowering and substantial. . . . The great sacramental experiences of baptism, confirmation, and eucharist then become the primary paradigms for blessing children, youth and adults and giving them a vision of their meaning, purpose and eternal destiny in life's pilgrimage.[5]

When I consider these three definitions of confirmation, I am struck by the implications for teaching and learning that they evoke. Brueggemann's article on confirmation was written in 1974. At that time, most churches spoke of this educational program as communicants' class, or education that was preparation for joining the church. For many churches and still for some today, to receive a welcome to the Lord's Table for the sacrament of communion, you first had to pass through the door of communicant's class. The separation of communion from church membership and the act of welcoming children to Christ's table began to take place about this time in the early 1970s.

Brueggemann suggests that church membership is a commitment to belonging and that joining the church is more than adding a name to the church rolls. He argues that the confirmation affirmation of a young person to belong to, for, and with is a decision to join a community of faith committed to the biblical story, joining with people who live with an alternative view of the world lived in response to Jesus' call to be his disciples, and choosing with others to live a life that is not easy, choosing to live the bothered life of a Christian, "joining a crunch".

As I worked during the school year of 2001–2002 with two confirmation teachers, the associate pastor of the church, and eighteen adults who agreed to work as mentors with youth in the confirmation class, I was struck by the truth of William Myers' statement that confirmation really is "a window into the faithfulness of congregational practice." Adults, with very busy lives of work and family, took time to be involved in the lives of young people, to meet to plan for teaching, to call a teenager and make plans for lunch together, or to meet over coffee and juice between church school and worship.

Bill Myers argues for an understanding of confirmation that moves it far beyond a class with a teacher and learners. The idea of confirmation as relationship between the confirmands and the congregation is also affirmed in the definition of Browning and Reed, which adds the importance of another essential relationship in the process of faith formation, the family. Browning and Reed place confirmation within a sacramental context. Water, food, and learning sustain the journey of faith and life.

From the experience of reading, thinking, and now teaching confirmation, I offer this definition: Confirmation is the opportunity a congregation has to bless the growth in faith of its youth. Nurtured as children in a faithful family, youth have in confirmation the chance to voice their belief and faith and to claim the promises of their baptism. In the act of confirming faith, youth are publicly commissioned for mission and ministry as faithful Christians in their congregation, their community, and in the world. It also offers the opportunity for adults to be involved in the lives of its adolescents as teachers, mentors, and friends. Welcoming adolescents into membership and commissioning them for faithful ministry in the church and in the world is an act of faith and hope.

I believe that confirmation should not be remedial Sunday school. It is not the time to cram information into the heads of teenagers. This model assumes that youth have learned nothing from years of participation in church school and the larger life of the congregation. The liturgical scholar, Gail Ramshaw, has made a distinction between theology and liturgy: theology is prose, she says, but liturgy is poetry:

> If faith is about facts, then we line up the children and make them memorize questions and answers. . . . But if we are dealing with poetry instead of prose, . . . then we do not teach answers to questions. We memorize not answers but chants of the ordinary; we explain liturgical action . . . we immerse people in worship so that they, too, become part of the metaphoric exchange.[6]

Ramshaw is right; faith is so much more than facts. Confirmation is a time to engage youth in dialogue, to affirm beliefs, and to allow space for questions. It is an opportunity to ask them to be in worship with their family, to listen, observe, and share their experiences, even their critical comments.

In thinking about adolescents who leave the church at the first opportunity when given the choice, Kathleen Norris has said, "I wonder if children don't begin to reject poetry and religion for similar reasons because the way both are taught takes the life out of them. If we teach children when they're young to reject their epiphanies, then it's no wonder that we end up with so many adults who are mathematically, poetically, and theologically illiterate."[7]

How do we teach teenagers so that they will claim their epiphanies and name and claim the faith that is theirs? Confirmation does not have to be boring, relying on only one or two methods of teaching and learning—lecture or presentation and discussion. Nor does teaching and learning in confirmation have to be confined to a classroom model taught by the pastor. Bill Myers advocates for a teaching team of older youth and adults who plan and teach together. William Willimon has written curriculum for a mentoring model, one adult and one youth working together outside the box of a classroom.

Pastors are experimenting with varieties of models for confirmation in ways that strengthen both the content and the processes of teaching and learning and most importantly use methods of teaching and learning that do not bore youth to death. Many confirmation programs require each youth to complete a service project at some time during their participation in the class.

Some are moving confirmation out of the box of a separate class for teenagers and offering opportunities for youth to engage in learning with adults. At Immanuel Presbyterian Church in Milwaukee, confirmation takes place with juniors and seniors in high school. Most recently, the Reverend Dr. Deborah Block began their time together by asking them about the questions they had about faith. Their responses became the focus for house-church gatherings on Wednesday evenings during Lent. The series was entitled, "Faith Questions, What Difference Does It Make?" Each member of the confirmation class worked with an adult in the church in hosting the gathering and leading the discussion on their particular faith question in the context of worship. The questions of faith identified by the youth were: What difference does it make—to belong to a church? how we interpret the Bible? to be a Presbyterian? to believe in God? to be a Christian?

A Lutheran pastor was disturbed at the decline in participation in worship in the church and the lack of involvement by families in programs of Christian education. He decided to offer a mid-week class on the Bible that confirmands were required to attend with a parent or another adult. He has been amazed by the response, which has been mostly positive, and the resulting increasing participation in worship. He believes that offering the chance for parents and kids to learn about the Bible together helps dispel the fear of parents who believe they don't know enough.[8]

At Wildwood Presbyterian Church in Illinois, Co-pastor Greg Bostrom invites an adult to be a partner in faith with a youth who is participating in confirmation education. During the five months the class meets, each youth and adult partner-in-faith share the following experiences: Reading the Gospel of Luke and meeting every two weeks for conversation; worshiping together at least four times and discussing the experience; attending a church board meeting together and examining the church budget to see where the money goes; working together at a Christian service project and talking about why Christians reach out to others; working together on the confirmand's faith statement; and participating in the confirmation service.

These stories also reflect the idea that confirmation education does not have to be totally dependent on published curriculum. They illustrate what Maria Harris believes, that the designing of curriculum is "an artistic educational work" that contributes to the "fashioning of a people."[9]

What Precedes and What Follows in Religious Education

What if planning for confirmation education began with these questions instead of starting with the answers offered in the denominational confirmation curriculum used by your church? What if the setting for this conversation was a gathering of the pastor/educator, confirmation teachers, and parents of youth who would be participating in confirmation?

1. What have these youth been learning in church school prior to confirmation? What biblical stories and themes have they had a chance to explore? What other settings for religious education have contributed to their knowledge and experience of the Christian faith?

2. In what ways have they experienced the church in worship, mission, and ministry within its doors and in the community?

3. In what ways has their faith been formed at home with their family?

Too often confirmation education proceeds without considering these kinds of questions. It has been taught as remedial Sunday school, attempting through memory requirements and quizzes to cram into a young person a certain body of information. When taught in this way, the foundation of faith established in preschool and elementary church school experiences is ignored. The question of what is an appropriate transition from elementary curriculum to confirmation curriculum is not addressed.

Mainline denominations (for example, the United Church of Christ, Presbyterian Church [U.S.A.], United Methodists, or Lutherans) make content decisions easy by offering well-written confirmation curriculum. This is a real blessing in disguise. It is important for congregations to evaluate confirmation curriculum in terms of its appropriateness for their particular context.

Essential in designing programs of confirmation education are knowing what precedes and what follows in the church school. The kind of intentional thinking and planning that goes into a Christian education curriculum for elementary-age children in grades 1–6 also needs to be in place with youth during and after confirmation.

In preparation for writing a ten-month confirmation curriculum to use with eighteen seventh and eighth graders, I learned that for three years these young people had been involved in a rotation model of church school for elementary-age children that their church called the Peaceable Kingdom.[10] This information was incorporated into the planning of the content of the curriculum. The goal for learning was written to take into account what went on before the beginning of confirmation education.

Models of confirmation education in terms of length of the program and age of the participants vary widely among and within denominations. Lutherans generally have the longest program, which is at least two years for middle-school youth (grades 7–9). Presbyterians, Methodists, and UCCs have curriculum designed for a nine-month (school year) program. The age of participants varies depending on the practice of the congregation. Some offer it in middle school (grades 7–8), while others believe that confirmation education is more appropriately offered with older youth in senior high (grades 9–12).

Whenever confirmation education is offered in your congregation, it is essential to consider what follows it. What learning opportunities are offered for youth once they are confirmed? Curriculum for youth is available in all mainline denominations. It is important for someone to see the larger picture and how content and processes of learning are integrated from first grade through twelfth grade.

A helpful guide is to think about curriculum in terms of form, not printed paper. Maria Harris has suggested that curriculum is visible in the life of a congregation: in settings for teaching, learning, and worship; in times when the faith community comes together; in mission and outreach in the community; and in proclamation.[11] Curriculum goes even beyond these five forms. Curriculum "is the entire course of the church's life."[12]

In thinking about what follows confirmation, these questions could help guide the planning for continuing the religious education of youth:

1. What curriculum was used with these youth prior to this time? What biblical content, issues, and themes have they been engaged with in elementary and middle school?

2. What would Christian education for older youth look like if it was planned and designed around Maria Harris' five forms of curriculum—service and mission, prayer and worship, being in community, learning, and proclamation?

3. What theological issues about faith and life were raised in confirmation education that can become content for the future?

4. What model of Christian education works best with adolescents who are as varied in their learning styles as are adults? What if you thought outside the box of a classroom, table, and chairs? What if you thought about models of teaching and learning other than discussion? What learning styles are represented in this group of youth?

5. What adults in the church would be the best teachers for youth? Who in the congregation has a passion for teaching and, at the same time, enjoys being with teenagers?

These critical questions are offered in the hopes that congregational committees of Christian education, nurture, or youth ministry (however it is named in your church) can look at the whole cloth, in addition to the individual pieces. Churches that make a commitment to the Christian education of all their people offer a tapestry rich in potential for nurturing a life of Christian faith.

Confirmation Models—Considering Settings, Learning, and Teaching

What memories do you have of your own confirmation experience? How old were you? What, if any, meanings carried forward with you into adulthood? As you sit for a minute with your own reflections, consider these of poet and author Kathleen Norris:

> I had a radiant faith as a child, mostly related to song and story. Like many people of my "baby boomer" generation, I drifted away from religion when catechism came to the fore, and the well-meaning adults who taught Sunday school and confirmation class seemed intent on putting the vastness of "God" into small boxes of their own devising. Theirs was a scary vocabulary, not an inviting one. And religion came to seem just one more childhood folly that I had to set aside as an adult.[13]

Norris' memory of confirmation raises questions about purposes of confirmation education and the pedagogy that is used in teaching and learning with adolescents. In this short quote, notice her memory of the changes that happened for her in her transition from a child of faith to a teenager. What pedagogical differences account for the change in her faith that she describes as "radiant" to a faith that was represented by adults as scary and not at all inviting?

Denominational curriculum attempts to balance both content and processes of teaching and learning appropriate for a wide range of both younger and older youth. It is interesting to examine curriculum looking for the methods of teaching and learning that are suggested. Most rely heavily on cognitive models of thinking with a majority of learning activities that require oral/linguistic (discussion) and writing skills. These are certainly excellent ways to learn but they are not the only ways.

Howard Gardner is an educator whose work is greatly influencing what we know about learning. In his books, *Frames of Mind: The Theory of Multiple Intelligence*s and *Intelligence Reframed: Multiple Intelligences for the 21st Century*, Gardner argues that with the help of intelligence tests used in schools, we have defined intelligence in much too narrow terms:

> One can think of intelligence as an elastic band. . . . Until now, the term intelligence has been largely limited to linguistic and logical capacities, although humans can process other elements as diverse as the contents of space, music, or their own and others psyches. Like the elastic band, conceptions of intelligence need to encompass those diverse contents—and stretch even more. We must move beyond solving existing problems and look more at the capacities of human beings to fashion products (like works of art, scientific experiments, classroom lessons, organization plans) that draw on one or more intelligences.[14]

He proposes that we possess at least eight intelligences in differing levels of ability. Simply described they are:

1. Oral-linguistic—the ability to use words either in speaking or in writing

2. Logical-mathematical—the ability to use numbers and logic, to understand propositions and abstractions

3. Spatial—the ability to connect ideas with visual representation; artistic gifts as well as sensitivity to color and form

4. Bodily-kinesthetic—the ability to express one's self with one's body, also including the ability to create, design, or transform things with hands

5. Musical—sensitivity to sound, pitch, and melody as well as the ability to express, perform, compose, and appreciate music

6. Naturalist—a connection with the natural world, seeing one's own environment

7. Intrapersonal—the ability to know one's self—strengths and weaknesses; self-esteem

8. Interpersonal—the ability to relate to others, to perceive moods and feelings of others.[15]

Teachers using this theory in public school teaching learn to help children speak of their intelligence as where they have strengths and where they have weaknesses, areas for growth and development. Gardner's theory has been widely adapted in curriculum planning for elementary schools.

Neil MacQueen is a Presbyterian minister who first became interested in the possibilities for using computers in religious education. Then working with other religious educators, he began to raise questions about the implications of Gardner's theory of multiple intelligences for church school education. The Workshop Rotation Model of Christian Education was the result of this thinking and collaboration with other educators who were concerned about kids and learning about the faith and the related issue of the difficulty in finding adults who felt competent and willing to teach.

Traditional classrooms with a teacher or teachers working with a specific grouping of elementary age children and focusing on a different biblical story each week is totally transformed in the workshop rotation model. Rooms become workshops and are named according to the intelligence that is used in engaging with the biblical story. One biblical story is learned and experienced for four-to-six weeks, depending on the number of workshops a church uses. Kids rotate by grade or grouping among the different workshops. A teenager or adult who is their shepherd moves with them from workshop to workshop while the teachers stay in the room. Some workshops are considered standard for churches using this model of church school. Churches usually give them names to help the children remember where they are working and learning on a particular Sunday. Here are some examples:

1. Art Room—Thou Art

2. Movie Room—Let There Be Lights

3. Computer Room—Bug Bytes

4. Drama Room—The Room of Acts

5.   Service/Mission—Seeds of Faith

6.   Cooking or Music can also be a separate workshop—One church calls their sixth room "The Eighth Day of Creation" and the learning style changes according to the biblical story that is being taught.

This model has cut across denominational lines. At its earliest stage of development in 1990, churches were encouraged to write their own curriculum. Potters Workshop and Cornerstones are the names of curriculum written for workshop rotation by Christian educators and pastors, and they served as a model for curriculum writing.[16] Now ELCA (Evangelical Lutheran Church in America) writes and sells *Firelight* and UMC (United Methodist Church) has produced *Power Express*.

The Workshop Rotation Model has been adopted as a church school model for the most part with elementary grades, first through sixth. Some churches are experimenting with the model with middle-school-age youth (sixth to eighth grades). A challenge for those who teach and are in ministry with adolescents is considering the theory of multiple intelligences and how it might be addressed in confirmation education and church school for youth after confirmation. This is an important issue for those churches who are using a workshop-rotation church school with elementary-age children. If kids have been working with biblical text, themes, and implications of text for living in ways that engage all their intelligences and abilities, what happens when they make a transition to a model of teaching and learning that involves sitting around a table and talking for an hour? For some youth this is easy, for other more kinesthetic learners, it is extremely difficult.

There are three basic models of confirmation education. Many congregations use a traditional classroom model with youth working with one or two teachers that may or may not include the pastor. Some classes meet for one hour during the church school time on Sunday. Others meet mid-week. Some follow an intensive model with retreats and longer sessions on Saturdays. Oftentimes this model follows the school year, August or September through May or June with confirmation taking place on Pentecost Sunday.

The second model moves confirmation education out of a schooling model into a mentoring model. In this type of program, an adult is paired with a confirmand and they work together one on one. In commenting about this model, Willimon has said that it grew out of a discussion in a Christian education committee in response to his confession about the Thursday afternoon confirmation-schooling model and why it wasn't working for him or the teenagers. In wondering about how they could design something better than what they had, the committee discussed their hopes for confirmation. "All we want is a dozen youth who, in their beliefs and lives, come to look like our best Christians."[17] Then they agreed on four principles:

1. The goal of confirmation is discipleship.

2. Learning about being a disciple requires more than learning knowledge and facts about Christ. "Confirmation class should do nothing less than equip young people to be disciples."[18]

3. Growing into the life of being Christian is a lifelong process and confirmands have already begun this journey. "Christianity is much more than a "head trip"; it is a way of life together. . . . Confirmation continues and strengthens Christian growth, already begun."[19]

4. "Most of us become Christians by looking over someone else's shoulders, emulating some admired older Christian, taking up a way of life that was made real and accessible through the witness of someone else."[20] Confirmation can be a time for teenagers to spend time with mentors, to look over the shoulders of another Christian.

Making Disciples is the curriculum William Willimon wrote for this model, which grew out of a confession of frustration and subsequent creative thinking with laypeople about what would really help youth grow in their experience of the meaning of being a disciple of Jesus. This model seems to work well in congregations who have a small number of youth participating in confirmation education. This model can also be adapted by having some occasions for common gatherings in addition to the one-on-one times when mentor and confirmand get together. Essential for the success of this model is a group of committed adults who agree to be mentors, a group who agree to spend time with a teenager and to spend time together in preparation and reflection.

A third model combines elements of the other tw
and an opportunity for adult mentoring, as well as
adults in the congregation. The stories on pages 74–
amples. The learning connections with other adults hap
ited time and does not take the place of an essential comp ....t in confirmation education—time and space for youth to learn, question, and
discuss with their peers and teachers. For an example of a model of
confirmation education that combines individualized and communal
learning, see Appendix 8.

How can we make Christian education for adolescents as interesting and challenging as the ways they are learning in their school settings? I have been intrigued with the ways that elementary children are
given independent projects for completion over a period of time. I was
sitting in the room with my nephew while he was working on the computer, and he started talking about Ansel Adams photography and which
were his favorite pictures. Russell was working off a Web site and showed
me the pictures he liked best and asked if I had ever seen them. After I
expressed my curiosity about his sudden interest in Ansel Adams, he
showed me his project assignment.

For a fifth-grade assignment in his math class, he was required to
complete a project on the life and work of Ansel Adams. It included five
parts: using computers and the Internet to learn information about his
life and work as a photographer and environmentalist; a report based on
the research; after viewing Adams' photographs, select a favorite in representation of three categories—nature, people, and a mathematical principle (lines or geometric shapes) and print one from each category; using a camera (standard, Polaroid, or digital) take a picture that shows
contrasts of light and dark and include this picture in the report; design
a cover for the report with an appropriate illustration.

Earlier he had gone outside with a camera loaded with black and
white film and shot a number of pictures of trees and then selected the
ones to include with his project. While we were talking, he selected and
then printed the pictures from the Web site and included them with his
report.

Like the quote from Kathleen Norris earlier in this chapter about
the way we teach math and poetry, any confidence I had about math
was eliminated early in my schooling because of the way it was taught. I
became very excited about my nephew's assignment because of the integration of a variety of processes of teaching and learning used in this

ith assignment. Then I thought about the connection between this assignment and teaching and learning with youth in confirmation.

Imagine a confirmation class with curriculum designed for a workshop-rotation model. It's a ten-month model (August through May) and includes these foci:

August–September (three weeks)—Group building, who we are as learners together

September (two to three weeks)—The Bible—the story of who we are

October—Beginning focus on the Trinity and the nature of God

November—Focus on the work of God as Spirit

December—Focus on Jesus

January—The church and other faith traditions, what makes us alike, what makes us different

February—Worship and sacraments in our tradition

March—Confirmation projects, A time for youth to work individually or with a partner on a project of her or his choice. See Appendix 7 for a project list I used. The meeting with the officers prior to their confirmation became a time when each confirmand shared his or her confirmation project, and the officers were encouraged to engage in dialogue with them about why they had selected the project and what they had learned.

April—Here I stand; creeds and confessions of the church and my/our faith statement

May—The church and mission

Consider the Ansel Adams assignment and how that might translate into a four-week rotation on the life and work of Jesus with the goal of becoming familiar with who Jesus was from the perspective of the gospel writer Matthew with a particular focus on the work of Jesus as teacher, healer/miracle worker, radical/defiler, and Savior/Messiah. These rotations could be divided among rooms if such space is available. Or two "rooms" could be set up in the same place. Or if the group is small, they could work in one "room" each week.

Movie Room—View and discuss a video such as *Parables That Jesus Told*, narrated by Garrison Keilor, or, *How to Get Blessed without Sneezing*, a video that explores the meaning of the Beatitudes.

Art Room—Several options could be offered in one room: have religious art books available such as *The Faces of Jesus* or the Lectionary art books from *Imaging the Word*, United Church of Christ curriculum.[21] Invite the youth to find art that reveals the different roles of Jesus, selecting the ones she or he likes best; have Bibles available and a variety of art forms—clay, watercolors, colored pencils, colored markers, oil paints—and invite the youth to illustrate a story about the life or work of Jesus as told in the gospel of Matthew. Or have cloth squares available to make a banner.

Computer Room—Have Web sites identified so the youth could view photographic or artistic representations of the life of Jesus.

Hands of Faith—Have copies of church newsletters and bulletins from the past six months available and invite the youth to use colored highlighters to note places where they see the work of Jesus going on in the life and ministry of this congregation. Where are there opportunities for learning about the Bible; where are places of healing and growth; where are there opportunities to serve in places of mission in the name of Jesus; where are their radical acts of witness, places where the church takes a stand in the name of faith? Use a different color for a role of Jesus that is embodied in the life of the congregation. Another option would be to actually have a project for the youth to complete, one that connects them to mission priorities of the congregation.

A Cloud of Witnesses—The Faithful Adults Who Surround Teenagers

One innovation in confirmation curriculum in the last twenty years has been the concept of inviting adults to serve as mentors or faith partners for youth who are involved in a program of confirmation education. When I worked as an educator in three congregations in the early 1980s, I had the chance to design and teach a confirmation class. One part of the program that I was most concerned to change for many educational reasons was the examination of the young people by the officers of the church. It had become something the youth hated and dreaded. The idea that they would be asked questions individually seem to hang over their heads all through the year.

That year we decided to change several things. The first focused on the design of the meeting with the officers prior to confirmation. In years past, I had observed officers sitting around a table in the "Session Room" with the youth seated behind them around the walls. For the meeting with the officers we moved from their space to the youth room. Chairs for each youth were set in a semicircle in front of the officers. At the beginning of the class in the fall, I had asked each youth to select one adult to serve as their sponsor. These sponsors were invited to one of their class sessions and we talked about what it meant during this year to be working together.

This meeting with the officers began with each adult sponsor standing behind a young person and introducing her or him to the session. I still remember the words of one of my friends saying, "This is Kathy, I have known her family for many years and I remember the day she was born and the day she was baptized." As I watched each adult proudly introducing a teenager, I hoped that each one would remember this moment.

Before confirmation curriculum began to include the concept of adult mentors, William Myers discussed the role of an adult who works with youth as a guarantor, who is a

> kind of living wilderness marker, one who stands as an adult but who also helpfully walks with a youth on his or her journey. Guarantors share the burden of the journey, help read the road maps, raise the hard questions of faith, and offer needed encouragement. They incarnate "adultness" in ways that encour-

age young people to grow. They embody the faith in a variety of forms. In this way, they "guarantee" the good news that adulthood is feasible and that the Christian story is also their story.[22]

Many congregations have a core of faithful adults who are willing to teach teenagers and work with them in programs of mission and youth ministry. These same congregations have many adults who also would say, "Don't ask me to teach teenagers. That's not something I can do!" A confirmation mentoring program that matches a faithful adult with a confirmand is a way both to involve more adults and to include adults across the life span (young adults, middle-aged, and older) in relating to youth in the congregation.

In writing about his church's use of mentors or faith partners in confirmation education, Reverend Greg Bostrom has said that the faith partners are the best part of the class. "I recruit an adult partner for each kid (I don't ask for volunteers, I handpick them) and ask them to commit to doing several activities together, one on one, as they prepare for confirmation. While it's a fairly significant commitment, nearly everyone says "yes" when I ask them. It says something about how people are willing to make commitments when they recognize the importance of the task."[23] Greg also asks church members to serve as prayer partners for a youth. The identity of the prayer partner is revealed to each youth on the Sunday of confirmation.

Week in and week out, children, youth, and adults see each other at juice and coffee hour at church and worship beside each other. Children play with each other, youth talk together, and adults check in with other adults. We naturally segregate by age. Confirmation mentoring programs offer youth for whom church is not a choice to have conversations with adults for whom faith and active participation in a congregation is not just their choice, it is a priority for their life.

In 2001, when I was actively involved with a congregation and their confirmation education program, we invited the confirmation mentors to a lunch and orientation session after worship one Sunday. These were all very busy adults in their work life and in their church life. When talking about hopes for their work as mentor, one adult said that when she was called and invited to be a mentor, she agreed because she remembered the adult who had served as a mentor for her own daughter and how important that relationship had been.

One religious concept very popular in writing today is that of spirituality or spiritual practices. As was mentioned in Chapter 2, spiritual practices are the very daily things we do that nurture and sustain a life of faith. In talking with the adults at their orientation session, we encouraged them to think of this mentoring relationship as a spiritual practice. For six months, they would be thinking about, talking with, and praying for one particular teenager in their church.

In his confirmation mentoring curriculum, William Willimon wrote this definition: "A mentor is one who has a genuine faith and who is involved in trying to grow in that faith from day to day. A mentor is one who is willing to share his or her journey of faith with another person."[24] The opportunity for a teenager to "look over the shoulder" of an adult in the church who is not their parent, their confirmation teacher, or their youth group leader gives them the experience of getting to know another person in the church and perhaps see the Christian faith as it is lived through the witness of their life.

Some things to remember when using a mentoring model with youth in confirmation or youth preparing for baptism are:

1. Think carefully about the match between the teenager and the adult and the interests they may share. Consider a variety of adults across the life span in the congregation.

2. When inviting adults to serve as mentors, be clear about the expectations involved in this mentoring relationship. It is better to accept an honest no from someone than a less than enthusiastic yes.

3. Plan a get-together with the mentors for some orientation. Appendix 5 is an example of a handout to use at such a time. One way to do this is to gather for a simple lunch after worship. Spend a few minutes talking about each youth and then review the handout and the expectations for mentoring.

4. Periodic checking in with the mentors over the course of the year is also a good idea as well as giving the youth a chance to say what they have been doing with their mentors. Plan at least one or two gatherings during the year for mentors and youth together. Sometimes it helps adult mentors connect with others and plan things to do together. Some adults can quickly think

of many things to do with their teenager while others need help with ideas. Working on a service project together is a great way.

Blessing, Affirmation, Confirmation, and Commissioning for Faithful Living

It is Pentecost Sunday, a time of remembering the gift of God's Spirit (Acts 2:1–21). Pentecost is a day of celebrating the beginnings of the Christian church and remembering the ways Jesus welcomed all people. Many congregations also have the tradition of welcoming confirmands into the church on Pentecost Sunday. For youth who have been participating in a class or mentoring program, it marks the transition to affirming faith and claiming for themselves the identity and vocation of being Christian.

Just as a church is forever changed when it welcomes children, youth, and adults at their baptism, a congregation is also changed by the welcoming of confirmands. Three people have made important comments on the reality of these changes. Myers has said that:

> The church that recognizes the tension existing between the expectations of our culture and the covenantal significance of baptism can begin to understand confirmation as a rite that confirms a personal acceptance by the confirmand of baptismal vows, carrying an accompanying increase in the ministerial responsibilities of new community members, and affirming—in real ways—the vocation of both its adolescent and adult believers. Viewed in this fourfold fashion, the covenantal faithfulness of a church is suspect to the degree that it fails to accept and integrate into the congregation those adolescents and adults who complete such a faithful process.[25]

Janet Fishburn believes that "if infant baptism, the confirmation of baptismal vows, and new member rituals do not require a potential 'member' to know, do, or be anything in particular, no one should be surprised that congregations lack spiritual vitality."[26] Carol and Larry Nyberg wonder about the exodus of teenagers from the church and ask two essential questions, "Could it be that the church has left them? Have we searched enough to find food for their growing, stretching hearts?"[27]

These educators speak to a number of issues: the content and processes of teaching and learning, the connection of confirmands to the congregation, and what happens after confirmation. In speaking about the "covenantal faithfulness of a church," a congregation's "spiritual vitality," and the food required for "growing, stretching hearts," they address a central issue of the integration of Christian education and vocation. This integration is required of the whole congregation, not just those youth who are being confirmed or affirmed.

The title of the last section of this chapter reveals the choices available to youth, their families, and the congregation—blessing, affirmation, confirmation, and commissioning for faithful living. In an earlier book, *Come unto Me: Rethinking the Sacraments for Children*, I told the story of two colleagues who struggled with the honest confession of youth participating in confirmation class who did not want to be confirmed. They knew it was important to honor the decision of youth themselves and support this decision in dialogue with the families. As a result of their experiences with youth who were not yet ready to make a public profession of Christian faith, Affirmation Sunday was created, which happens the Sunday before youth are confirmed. Youth choosing affirmation receive a blessing for their participation with the class and are affirmed for their continued growth in the life of the Christian faith.

In teaching confirmation education, it is essential to make room for those youth who are not yet ready for confirmation. By knowing in advance the kids who choose to be confirmed and those who choose to wait, there is time to plan for both the affirmation and the confirmation that will take place in worship. Whether a youth chooses to be affirmed or confirmed, they should be blessed and commissioned for the next steps in their living of the Christian faith.

Ways to Celebrate Confirmations and Affirmations

Many congregations try to make the Sunday of confirmation a special day so that youth, their families, and the extended family of faith will remember the vocation to which they are all called, that of being Christian. Consider these ideas for ways to celebrate confirmations and affirmations.

With the Faith Community

1. **Involve children in the church school**—Children can make cards and bookmarks to give to those being confirmed and affirmed.

2. **Involve parents and mentors**—Ask them to write or to make something for their teenager. Here's an example:

Would you write or make something for your teenager? It could be a story about your own faith journey; an expression of your hope or wish for them on this special day; something about their baptism that you want him or her to remember; something about your own faith in God and what that has meant to you; a favorite Bible verse and why it is important to you; or something about the ways you are involved in the life, work, and ministry of this church and what this has meant to your own life of the Christian faith. This writing could be in the form of a letter, poem, or journal entry. It could also be a piece of art—a drawing, painting, quilt square, collage, a bookmark to use in their Bible. Selecting a card and giving that is also a fine idea.

3. **Faces of faith**—What about creating a confirmation wall that has a group picture of each confirmation class. It's a great way to remember the youth and their contribution to the life of the congregation. Include a copy of the picture and information about the youth in the next issue of the church newsletter.

In Worship

4. Consider the parts of worship where members of the confirmation class can share their gifts of leadership as liturgists, musicians, or artists.

5. **Liturgy**—The call to worship, confession of sin, and prayers can be written for this service as part of the confirmands' study of worship. Some churches have the tradition of each member of the class writing a confirmation statement. These statements

could be printed in a small booklet and distributed with the bulletins. Faith statements can also be created in forms other than written words, such as a piece of music written in response to a biblical text or a banner, collage, or drawing. These offerings can be used in worship and for a cover for the bulletin. Other churches work with the confirmation class in writing a group faith statement. This could be printed in the bulletin and used as the statement of faith for all to read together in worship.

6. **Recognizing gifts and talents**—In addition to being affirmed for their time of study and growth in faith and being confirmed into membership of a church, youth can also be commissioned for particular ways they want to share their time and talents with their congregation. This could be printed in the bulletin or read to the congregation.

7. **Gifts from the congregation**—Congregations have their own traditions for recognizing steps of faith and life. Infants or children who are baptized are given a cradle cross, a book, a cross-stitch with the date of their baptism, or a book for their parent or parents. Congregations mark a child's beginning ability to read by giving him or her a Bible storybook. Bibles are given to youth at their confirmation. Some congregations mark the beginning of confirmation with the gift of a Bible so it can be used during the course of the class and then give a colorful wooden cross from Central America at the end of the class. Confirmation candles are also a gift that could be given. Confirmation certificates signed by the pastor and the teachers will help the youth and his or her family to remember this day.

At Church and Home

8. Plan a lunch after worship for the confirmation class and their family and friends. If the weather is warm, a picnic outside at church if there is room or at the home of one of the church members would be a great way to gather for a final celebration. A meal at tables in the large room in the church works equally well. Gifts made by the children and gifts from parents and mentors could be on the tables marking the place for the youth.

9. Plan a family meal sometime during the week or weekend of Affirmation or Confirmation Sunday to celebrate this day. Perhaps the one being honored could select the menu. If a child has a close friend in the confirmation class, a joint celebration could be planned. If additional family members or friends from out of town are coming for this day, they could be invited to bring cards or letters to give to the youth. Friends or family members who can't be there for this special day can be asked to send a letter or card.

10. **Remembering the day**—Make a scrapbook. Some families like to collect pictures and stories and put together a scrapbook for special occasions. Another way to remember this day is to light a confirmation candle on the anniversary each year and take some time to recall the year and the way everyone in the family has shared his or her time and talents in the church. Pentecost, the liturgical celebration of the gift of God's Spirit as told in Acts 2:1–21, which is observed fifty days after Easter, is also a great occasion to recall confirmation stories.

A Psalm of Thanksgiving—Psalm 65

Read Psalm 65, which is described as a community song of thanksgiving that was used in Israel's worship at times of major festivals at the Temple. What is David, the author of this poem, saying about God?

Walter Brueggemann has written about the practice of praying the psalms, which he says depends on two things: (1) what we find in the psalms when we read them and (2) how we connect with the psalm out of our own life experiences. "The work of prayer is to bring these two realities together—the boldness of the Psalms and the extremity of our experience—to let them interact, play with each other, tease each other and illuminate each other. . . . All this is to submit to the Holy One in order that we may be addressed by a Word that outdistances all our speech."[28]

Spend some moments praying with this psalm. What do you find in this psalm? In what ways does it relate to experiences in your life, experiences in your life with teenagers?

5

A Backpack of Belonging

I have always been amazed by people who know how to pack for a trip. Now perhaps it has more to do with differing standards of what is enough than it does with folding and layering clothes. I think we all probably fall into two categories—stuffers and nonstuffers. I confess I'm in the first category. I can never decide what to take. I like options. My sister and I went to England when she was in college. We met in Atlanta the night before we left. She took one look at my suitcase, dumped everything out, and told me I could take half of what I had packed. I recently solved the problem of stuffing by buying one of those twenty-six–inch suitcases on wheels that you can check. It holds enough for a week for me, two weeks for everyone else. Since I was going to Maine for a week, I thought it would be perfect to travel with one bag, checked all the way through. Of course, my bag was one of two that did not make it to Maine with all the others.

I believe that part of the fear of parents when it comes to teenagers is the concept of "good-enough."

- Have I been a good-enough parent?

- Will my child remember and value what we have been teaching him?

- Have I taught her everything she needs to know about the world?

- I want her to love God and the church and I want faith to be important to him, but I don't know what he thinks!

- Does my teenager even listen to what I say or care what I think?

- What will he take with him when he leaves home? What will she leave behind?

- Have we been a good-enough family?

- Is our home a place to which they will want to invite their friends?

- How many times do I have to look at his rolling eyes before it's okay to say, enough already?

We hope that by the time they are eighteen and leave home for college, jobs, or families of their own, we have stuffed enough in their backpacks, so to speak, that they will contain everything they need to see them through the journey to adulthood. Surely that is the wish of every parent of a teenager. We worry, we hope, we pray a lot, and we worry some more and pray some more that this beloved child will grow up and do good in this world; that they will remember the words of the prophet Micah who wrote that what the Lord requires is this: to do justice, and love kindness, and walk humbly with your God.

We like to think that if we give them a quick injection of a magic potion of love and kindness, a moral and faithful compass somewhat like a booster shot, that's what will see them through. Of course, when we start panicking about this border crossing, and we remember going through it ourselves, we know that everything we have done to this point matters.

When I worked with youth as a church educator, parents of a teenager said to me that they would love to get their child to come to the youth group, but they were having a hard time. Knowing the family, I wasn't surprised. Church had never been a priority in their lives. Other activities of the children took precedence. Family participation in worship, education, mission, and service is a habit of the heart that forms a family in faith. It can't begin at age thirteen.

There are people who I think offer some frames for thinking about a backpack of belonging for our young people. A few years ago, Bill and Barbara Myers wrote an important book about children, *Engaging in Transcendence: The Church's Ministry and Covenant with Young Children.*

In that book, they identified four core conditions that characterize effective Christian ministry with children. Ministry occurs when adults are caring presences, capable of providing hospitality in which the child's contextual experience is honored and transcendence is expected.

I think these core conditions also need to be present in our living with teenagers at home and in the congregation. The implications are obvious. We honor who young people are and remember that the physical, social, and mental changes that they are experiencing are normal. Our job is to be a caring presence, one that remembers the difficulty of this age yet holds them accountable to life within the family. When we expect transcendence, we watch with an attitude of expectancy and hope. The Myers' say that the word "transcendence" "points at the process of moving over, going beyond, across, or through real or imagined limits, obstacles or boundaries."[1]

I think the one difference in applying these core conditions to adolescents is that they become more mutual than one way. In being caring and loving presences with adolescents, they will learn how to be and do that with others. When we model hospitality for and with them, they learn how to extend that to another. Just like a two year old, the developmental task of the adolescent is to make their voice heard, to make their own choices about when they say no and when they say yes. But teenagers are at a different stage cognitively. They are able to reason and to understand the point of view of another. So they can understand about honoring the context and experience of their family, a parent or grandparent who have needs just like them. And surely transcendence happens within families as children move through adolescence.

The other person who I think offers some insight for this age group is Mary Pipher. She wrote about the six things that shelter families in her book *The Shelter of Each Other: Rebuilding Our Families*, which was discussed in Chapter 3. Her thesis is that if a family is to be strong, it must "build walls that give the family definition, identity and power."[2] A family that builds on a foundation of faith beginning at birth or adoption names that which is the source of the strength of the family.

Ten Things Youth Need

As our young people cross the borders from childhood to adolescence and then to young adulthood, they need some resources for the journey. When I think of a symbol of adolescents today, their backpacks immediately come to mind. Think of the resources inside them in terms of a "backpack of belonging."

What are these things we would stuff in their backpacks, so to speak? What are the values, the experiences we hope adolescents will remember as they move through this time of their life on their way to adulthood? I think of ten things that are provided by a teenager's family and faith community.

1. Placemats, Blessings, and Family Time

Think about the dining table around which a family gathers for meals. What shape is it? Where do people sit? What sits in the middle of the table? If meals begin with a blessing, how is it done—spoken or sung, led by a parent or passed around to each member of the family? Do you hold hands during the blessing?

It's no surprise to say that in the culture in which we live, family time becomes a scarce and precious thing. As lives of busy adults and teenage children are divided between work and school, being with friends and activities after school and work, the available time for family shrinks to a matter of minutes. Family mealtime and conversation may happen on the average of two or three times a week.

Many family traditions begun with young children continue to work as the family grows older together—mealtimes, blessings, and conversations are some of those things. Another is the time a family spends together doing things it enjoys. What is it your family enjoys doing together—hiking, sports, listening to music, sharing news of the world and the day at mealtime, going to church together, watching movies, helping others, gardening, working jigsaw puzzles?

The Gospel of Matthew records Jesus' instructions to his disciples about prayer and told them to "pray in this way" and then gave them what we call the Lord's Prayer. This much loved and memorized prayer is simple in its form. It gives us a chance to praise God, to make a request of bread and forgiveness, and reminds us that we are also to forgive others.

We hope a child's backpack of belonging has a pocket available for memories of family time shared together around a table and beyond, memories of listening, being and doing things together, prayers at meals, and prayers during the day and evening.

2. Watermarks and Promises

A child is born or adopted into a family and promises are made at this child's baptism or dedication. The sacrament of infant baptism or the liturgical ritual of infant dedication offers a parent or parents and a congregation the opportunity to affirm their faith together and to make a public commitment to raising this child in the Christian faith. This occasion is often one of great joy, hope, and expectation as a faithful congregation welcomes the newest one with water and words of promise. This sacrament or ritual, I believe, marks a child for a life of faith. Or perhaps it's better to say, it has the potential to mark a child for a life of faith.

Some pastors and lay leaders have the experience of teaching youth in confirmation who were baptized as infants but who have not been brought back to church since that moment. For this young person, their family has reduced the sacrament to a social or cultural marker.

Adolescents who have been raised in the educational life and worship of a congregation have been nurtured in the Christian faith. The waters of baptism or the words of blessing marked the beginning of their life lived in faith. Such fortunate young people have experienced the faithful witness of a faith community and are able to begin to affirm their own faith. What was a hope and promise of their parents can now be named and claimed by the young person.

Baptism and dedication stories and pictures are appropriate in a backpack of belonging that travels with an adolescent as she or he moves through life. These images and stories help them remember who they are—their place in their family and whose they are—God's and their place in a family of faith. They, like the prophet Isaiah, will hear these words of the Lord, "I have called you by name, you are mine" (Is. 43:1).

3. Sabbath Habits and Spiritual Practices

For some families, sabbath is a habit of the heart and soul. Going to church, participating in church school, being in worship together is a family priority. For other families sabbath is understood as requirement, something we should do, something we make an hour of our time for each week if other things aren't more important, like sports. Daily spiritual practices like those described in chapter 2 are part of the lives of many families. Others rely on one or at most two hours on Sunday morning to feed their spiritual life.

In the book of 1 Kings, we hear the story of the prophet Elijah. His prophetic words and his triumph over the priests of Baal put him in great disfavor with Ahab and his wife Jezebel, and Elijah fled into the wilderness in fear of his life. He lay down to sleep and an angel awoke him and told him, "Get up and eat, otherwise the journey will be too much for you." Elijah did as the angel said and escaped to a cave on Mount Horeb, and it was there that he found God, not in the wind, the earthquake, or the fire but in the "sound of sheer silence" (1 Kings 19:12).

What symbol would you put in your teenager's backpack of belonging that helps him or her remember a commitment to practices of faith? After he left Beersheba, Jacob took a stone for his pillow and dreamed of God and God's presence with him. "Know that I am with you and will keep you wherever you go, and will bring you back to this land; for I will not leave you until I have done what I have promised you" (Gn. 28:15). A teenager I know keeps a prayer rock under his pillow. It is a simple piece of felt that covers a rock and was given to him as a child to help him remember his connection to God and to close each day with prayers, with a time of listening for God in silence.

4. Bread and Juice

Many teenagers have grown up taking communion since they were young children and really can not remember a time when they were not included at Christ's table. That is a wonderful thing, to grow up participating in the sacrament of eucharist within a family of faith. I have watched young children being carried forward for communion and given a bit of bread soaked in the juice and told, "Jesus loves you." Then a year later, this same child runs forward on her own and breaks off her own piece of bread and dips it in the cup.

The sacrament is about remembering God's faithful and loving gift of his son Jesus Christ. It is a story of the bread of life and the cup of the new covenant, a story that is ever new as we are fed at the table and move out into the world to be God's witnesses wherever we are. What better gift can we give our teenagers than to tuck a small loaf of bread and a juice box into their backpack of belonging, symbols of life, creation, salvation, hope, and promise. Perhaps when they find these small gifts, they will remember meals shared at the table in a faithful congregation. Perhaps they will remember the faces of the people with whom they have worshiped, served, and shared a meal. Perhaps they will remember that having been fed at the table, nourished within a faithful congregation, they are able to feed and serve others.

The Gospel writer Luke records the story of the risen Lord meeting his disciples on the road to Emmaus, and it was in the sharing of a meal, in the breaking of bread that "their eyes were opened and they recognized him." Surely in the daily breaking of bread, we can remember the one Jesus, who is the living bread.

5. More than Setting Up Tables—Opportunities in the Church to Share Their Time and Talents

Another way to engage this issue is to ask the question, In what ways are youth integrated into the total life of the congregation? Are the gifts and talents of youth welcomed and valued, or are youth segregated from the congregation with a program of youth ministry? Are youth invited to share their talents with music, the arts, computers, or are they only called on when someone needs tables and chairs set up for church family meals? Are there opportunities for youth to play and work with adults in the church?

Two obvious ways a church expresses its commitment to its young people is through opportunities for religious education in the church school and in youth ministry programs offered at times other than Sunday morning. These opportunities of Christian formation provide opportunities for learning in small group settings. Other opportunities, such as retreats, tours of denominational colleges, and mission trips, are important experiences that help youth continue in their learning about the ways that belief and living a life of faith are connected.

As part of confirmation education, one congregation has the practice of asking adults to volunteer to be an anonymous prayer partner for one of the youth. Their identity is revealed to the youth on confirmation Sunday.[3] I hope that as an adolescent moves through middle school and high school their backpack of belonging includes opportunities and experiences of both receiving and giving, of knowing in concrete ways the meaning of belonging to a church.

6. Story, Vision, and Crunch

In an article referred to in Chapter 4 of this book, biblical scholar Walter Brueggemann referred to confirmation as the act of joining a story, joining a vision, and joining a crunch. I hope that by the time a person is in high school, he or she has a working knowledge of the Bible and of stories of God's people told in the Hebrew and Christian scriptures, people such as Ruth and Naomi, Elijah and Abraham, David and Esther, Peter and Martha, Mary, the rich young ruler, the woman at the well, and the disciples.

If a teenager has grown up within the life, learning, and mission of a congregation, then she has been able to catch a vision for this congregation's living out of its faith in the community and in the world. She has seen the commitments it makes to welcoming all of God's people into worship and mission. She has brought her cans of food and donations of money to add to the soup pot on Souper Sunday. She has seen the ways that adults live out their commitments to be God's faithful disciples sharing their time and talents in the world.

Perhaps as their minds continue to develop, teenagers have gotten a glimpse of the crunch of the Christian faith, that the life Jesus calls us to is very different from that of the culture. In their maturing life and faith, they are able to reflect critically on the beatitudes and what it means to be blessed.

Tucked into another pocket of a backpack of belonging is a verse written on a small piece of paper. A Pharisee stopped Jesus and asked him which was the greatest commandment. Jesus quoted Deuteronomy 6:5, "You shall love the Lord your God with all your heart, and with all your soul, and with all your mind." Then he added a second, "You shall love your neighbor as yourself. On these two commandments hang all the law and all the prophets." Here is the heart of faith, the story, the vision, and the crunch—loving God and loving our neighbor.

7. Soup Pots, Hammers, Stories, and Conversations

I have a friend who is an associate minister with responsibilities for ministry with youth and their families. She believes in the importance of youth being involved in ministries of mission and service. A major component of her work with the youth in the church is planning, funding, and leading a weeklong mission trip every summer. Each summer a different place is selected, one where youth and adults can work together building, repairing, or teaching vacation Bible school, experiencing the hands-on practice of sharing time and talents with strangers.

Another congregation is part of a cooperative shelter ministry from November through April and invites homeless people from the streets to eat and sleep in their building one night a week. Adults, families, youth—everyone is invited to volunteer to share a meal with the guests and to help with the overnight hospitality.

For a Christmas present, a parent gave her children the gift of time to volunteer together one afternoon a week after school in a nearby day-care center, reading and playing with preschool children.

The prophet Micah affirmed that what the Lord requires of us is to do justice, to love kindness, and to walk humbly with our God (Mic. 6:8). The Bible stories of Jesus and the people he met, which we so hope our children will grow up knowing and remembering, become incarnated in experiences of giving of ourselves, of acting on behalf of others, of taking difficult stands in this world. We hope a backpack of belonging of a youth will contain memories and stories of justice, kindness, and humble walking with another.

8. House Key and Phone Card

One of the most familiar verses in the Hebrew Bible is the Great Commandment or the Shema found in Deuteronomy 6:4–9. The commandment to love God with all our heart, soul, and strength is one we are to pass on to our children. Teach this to your children, talk about it when you are at home and when you are away, when you lie down and when you rise. The expectations of the great commandment are lifelong. It is not as if it is some great mystery, inaccessible to humankind. Rather, the commandment to love God is very near, requiring simple, intentional, and faithful action on our part. The last part of the Shema gives some final instructions about their implementation. "Bind them as a sign on your hand, fix them as an emblem on your forehead, and write them on the doorposts of your house and on your gates."

There was a popular advertisement for a motel chain that ended with the phrase, "We'll leave the light on for you." One markers of adolescence is the freedom of going and coming within the limits of the "house rules." A rule of parents often heard by their children is, "Call if you decide to go somewhere different. Just let me know where you are."

When I have asked groups of adults what they would put in an adolescent's backpack, things they would want them to have or to remember, these two items are always on the list. Parents want their older children to know that home is always a place to which they can return, a place where they are always welcome. Families also want their teenage children to know that staying connected by phone is also important, that "no matter where you are, or whatever happens to you, just call home, we are here for you."

A house key and a phone card tucked in a backpack of belonging are symbols of a life lived within a loving family. The love and faith that have been nurtured in a growing child now become visible in their actions as they move out into the world as independent human beings.

9. Family Pictures

Two parents took their oldest child to college and eagerly awaited to hear from him about how his life was going. In the first conversation they had, their son had one request. He wanted a picture of their family dog. I laughed with them in their amusement at this request, not for pictures of the family, but for a picture of the beloved family pet. The faces we see every day become even more important when separation occurs.

If you could slip a small picture album into your teenager's backpack of belonging, what pictures would you include? Of course, there would be pictures of family members and family pets. Who else would be included? One reality of children maturing into adolescents is that their circle of friends gradually begins to widen. These can be friends of their own age and older—teachers at school, church members who know them by name, neighbors, or adopted grandparents.

I think I would slip into their backpacks a very small calendar, one of those kind you can make yourself with your computer or have made at a copier store. Each month has a different photograph and so twelve different pictures of family and friends important in the life of this young person could be inserted.

Psalm 78 tells of the goodness of God and reminds us of the commandment, not unlike Deuteronomy 6:4, that we are to pass on to the next generation stories of God. We are to teach each new generation as the psalmist says, "So that they should set their hope in God, and not forget the works of God" (Ps. 78:7). Perhaps in seeing the faces of those who love them, teenagers will remember the faith of their family and remember to set their hope in God.

10. Candles, Flashlights, and Prayers

When I travel, I always stick a votive candle and holder into my suitcase. Lighting a candle in the evening before going to bed is an entry for
me into meditation, reflection on the day, and a reminder of home. The
smell of a vanilla candle sweetens the room, wherever I may be. Watching the flickering flame, I say my prayers and give thanks to God for life
and another day.

I have noticed that when I travel with one of my nephews, he always packs at least two or three flashlights of different sizes. On some
occasions, they provide light for reading in bed or even once the flashlight gave us a path to find our way out of a darkened motel room when
the fire alarm came on and the power was shut off. Everyone knows Josh
always packs flashlights in his backpack, and so we have come to count
on him to always be prepared with light when we need it.

Light is a wonderful biblical image. In Psalm 27, David writes, "The
Lord is my light and my salvation; whom shall I fear?" The Gospel writer
John records Jesus saying, "I am the light of the world. Whoever follows
me will never walk in darkness but will have the light of life" (Jn. 8:12).

Make sure your teenager's backpack of belonging has a small flashlight attached to the zipper pull, a symbol of hope and a way of remembering that God indeed lights our path, helping us discern in the darkness, the way to go. Remember also to have your own flashlight nearby.
Light a candle in the darkness or shine the flashlight around the room
wherever you are and say your prayers for the person this child has been
and is becoming.

Packing for Yourself

What will you put in your backpack? I think the culture we live in provides some clues about what they think is essential: drugs to help parents endure their teenager; longer work hours to earn more money to
buy more and better things for their teenage children; nonstop entertainment; extra tutoring so youth can get into the best schools. The
culture in which we live values the now, the newest, and nurtures the
need for immediacy and instant gratification. Parents always want the
best for their children, and that is something that does not change.
Parenting in the culture today in a way requires a roadmap through the
myriad of choices available to youth today.

So what do you need to see you through these years of challenge and opportunity as you walk with a teenager through his or adolescence? Take a few minutes to think about your list, and then compare it with this one.

1. **A psalter**—The book of Psalms seems to have something to say for almost any occasion in life—for the times of great joy as well as the times of sadness, worry, or grief. It is truly a timeless piece of poetry that helps remind us that in every situation we may encounter, God is there.

2. **A journal**—I would pack a small journal and pen to write things to remember about this time in a teenager's life. Baby journals, which provide places for photographs and memories, are very common. Not so common are journals to mark the growth and development of a teenager. One parent kept a journal of her son's last year of high school and gave it to him as a graduation gift. He took it with him to college.

3. **A small photograph album**— The family Christmas picture each year for the years of middle school and high school would reveal the changes as a teenager matures from childhood to adulthood. Pictures of a teenager involved in the activities she or he loves would also be included. A baby picture and a confirmation picture would be needed as well.

4. **T-shirt**—Consider packing a T-shirt belonging to your teenager. Does she or he have a favorite? What picture or words are on it? What would a T-shirt you wore as a teenager have pictured or said? It is a T-shirt culture, so to speak, and this keeps us in touch with what's going on.

5. **A package of seeds**—Seed packets are available in gardening centers in late winter or early spring. The picture on the front provides an image of what the seeds inside have the potential of becoming. I would pack one of these seed packets in my backpack, and on a warm and sunny day, plant the seeds and enjoy watching them grow. They would remind me of the beginnings of life of teenagers I love and how they continue to grow and add their unique contribution to this world.

6. **Favorite mug for coffee or tea**—While looking at photographs, watching flowers bloom, or writing in a journal, I would be able to sip a favorite beverage alone or with a friend and remember coffee/tea conversations over the years, sharing stories, hopes, fears, and frustrations involved in raising children.

7. **Worship bulletin**—I would pack this because it reminds me that I am not alone in raising a teenager. A congregation surrounds faithful families and holds them within their arms of prayer and concern. A worship bulletin reminds us of nature and mission of ministry. The liturgy calls us to worship with music and words, dance and drama, art and symbols. The biblical texts and the prayers, poems, or quotes for preparation for worship can be meditation moments for a week.

8. **Cell phone**—Yes, I would put one in. It can be turned on and off, amazing, isn't it, just like at home with the other things that can connect us or separate us from each other—TVs, beepers, pagers. A reality of life with adolescents is keeping up with their comings and goings. Family calendars on the fridge keep up with individual and family commitments but a cell phone helps a teenager know they can always find us and they can always call home.

9. **Prayers**—I was in the home of a friend and noticed a small box on her coffee table. I admired it and she said it was her prayer box. In it she kept on small slips of paper the people for whom she was praying that day. As she would move through her home, she would touch the box and say her prayers. I think I would include a small box or tin in my backpack to remind me of the importance of prayer, not only of praying to God but also of time spent in listening for God.

10. **Candle or flashlight**—This is the only item that is the same for both backpack lists. Perhaps our flashlights mean we can find each other in the dark. Lighting a candle connects me to a time of meditation and prayer, which slows me down, turns me in the right direction, and helps me to remember whose I am and who I am called to be in this world.

A Backpack of Belonging—What Will You Put in It?

Families are formed in many ways today through birth and adoption. Adolescents may be raised with two birth parents or parent or parents who adopted them. Committed partners raise a birth child or an adopted child together. Divorced parents share custody of their teenagers during the week or weekend, and some adolescents grow up knowing, loving, and living with one parent. Extended families of grandparents or aunts or uncles provide a loving home for a teenager. Some godparents or baptism sponsors take on an important role in mentoring a teenager who needs another loving adult in his or her life. Families open their homes to the friends of their teenage son or daughter, and young people who may be seeking the attention of a caring adult find a welcome place. Teenagers can and will adopt another family when they need it.

In his novel *Plainsong*, Kent Haruf tells the story of the intertwining of lives in a small Colorado town and provides word images of family and belonging. Maggie Jones is a teacher at the local high school and is concerned about one of her students who is pregnant and needs a place to live. Maggie decides to make a request to two bachelor farmer brothers, the McPherons. She drives out to the farm and asks them to consider letting Victoria live with them during her pregnancy. Realizing that their response was one of silence, she left them to think about her request. After they had finished their chores, the brothers begin to discuss Maggie Jones' request:

> "All right," Harold said. "I know what I think. What do you think we do with her?
> "We take her in," Raymond said. " . . . Maybe she wouldn't be as much trouble."
> "I'm not talking about that yet," Harold said. He looked out into the gathering darkness. "I'm talking about—why hell, look at us. Old men alone. Decrepit old bachelors out here in the country seventeen miles from the closest town which don't amount to much of a good goddamn even when you get there. Think of us. Crotchety and ignorant. Lonesome. Independent. Set in all our ways. How are you going to change now at this age of life?"
> "I can't say," Raymond said. "But I'm going to. That's what I know."[4]

As adults, parents, family members, we have the ability to see the changes taking place within our teenagers. As we watch them grow in every way, we know that these changes both internal and external require changes in us as well. Of all the characters described in Haruf's novel, I think these three, Harold, Raymond, and Victoria, are my favorites. In moving in with two bachelor farmer brothers, Victoria was being asked to trust her life with two strangers. The request that came to the brothers required them to make drastic changes in their lifestyle. Maggie Jones asked them to make room in their daily routine not just for a young woman but for one who had been rejected by her family and who was facing alone the impending birth of her child. The inklings they had about the trouble she might bring were correct.

Consider the connections between this story and biblical stories. Think of the different people God called. No one was ever ready. Everyone had a good excuse. Recall the visit of the angel Gabriel to a young woman named Mary and the startling news this angel gave to her. In some ways it is the same news anyone receives when they hear they are going to become a parent. Everything will change. Nothing will be the same. The McPheron brothers did not think they were prepared or experienced enough to invite a homeless young woman into their home and their lives, but they decided to try.

In a different novel, *Evensong*, Gail Godwin tells the story of an Episcopal priest in a small parish in Virginia. Prior to becoming a rector, Margaret and her husband had lived at a residential school for adolescents. Margaret was on call for NP's one night—nightly prayers. If one of the kids wanted this, they wrote N.P. on a piece of paper and taped it to their door. One night, Margaret came to Josie's room. Josie was a bit leery of the Bible and anything religious. She didn't know the Lord's Prayer but after listening to the Twenty-third Psalm, she decided she liked that one because, "You're not begging for anything and you've got company. Someone's going with you." Margaret left a Bible with her and Josie did a quick analysis of "turn-off" psalms, ones in which the writer was too much of a whiner. She also didn't like the psalms that spoke of violent acts and asked, "How can cruel whiny stuff like this be in the Bible?"

Margaret told her, "Because the psalms were written by humans, and humans are a messy, contradictory lot. They grow up very slowly. The reason these psalms still speak to us is because the writers showed us ourselves as we are and yet put it in a larger container. They're reporting to God what's going on inside them at the moment. They rage and lament and give thanks and praise for their good fortunes and curse their enemies some more and blame God for abandoning them, but they also write down God's voice telling them things they need to know, telling them that they are loved and special. It's a mixed bag, but the point is it's all in a bag, bigger than they are, called God."

"I thought the Bible was supposed to be a book that told you how to be good," Josie responded. "No, [Margaret said] it's a record of a people keeping track of their relationship with God over a very long period of time."[5]

Here is another vignette about faith and relationships. Not having grown up religious, Josie came to the Bible with a fresh and honest critique, asking questions we have probably considered but maybe never verbalized. I can imagine Margaret pausing after hearing Josie's question, taking a deep breath, and deciding what answer she would give, kind of like the McPheron brothers. Margaret's answer to Josie is both an affirmation about who God is and what the Bible is and consequently who we are in relation to God.

Lovingly we add to our teenager's backpack of belonging the honest yet nervous affirmation of a Raymond McPheron who doesn't really know what is ahead of him in welcoming a young teenage woman into their home but who is willing to try to change to make it happen. We also add a strong affirmation of faith like Margaret spoke to Josie. A backpack of belonging can be full of doubts and questions, but it can also contain confirmations of faith and moving out in trust with God.

A Psalm of Trust—Psalm 121

Felipe Martinez's grew up in a family of faith. Family trips began with gathering in the hall before the front door with his father reading Psalm 121 and offering a prayer for their safe travels. Felipe is now a minister and any group leaving the church on a mission trip meets in the front hall and hears Psalm 121 read and then has a prayer before their going.

Psalm 121 is a song of trust, or an assurance of God's protection. What is your prayer of protection for teenagers? What is your psalm of trust in God? An ancient way of meditation on God's Word is *lectio divina,* or divine reading. Read the psalm three times. The first time, listen for one word that you think describes what the psalm is saying.

For the second reading, think of a phrase that summarizes the meaning of the psalm. For the third reading, think about what you hear God asking you to do. Allow time for silence and meditation between each reading.

6

Suggestions for Teaching and Resources

This book can be used with adults in the church—parents, leaders, and teachers of youth. Here are suggestions for using it as the basis for a four- or six-week discussion designed for one-hour sessions such as church school on Sunday morning or a mid-week setting. The sessions could also work in a weekend retreat setting or as a workshop for parents or leaders of youth.

Each session follows the same four-step process for teaching and learning: Gathering, Exploring, Connecting, Going. This is a process used in the confirmation curriculum of the United Church of Christ, *Affirming Faith: A Congregational Guide to Confirmation.* Having intentional ways to begin and end each session—with prayer, biblical text, expressions of joys and concerns—affirms the value of the nature of teaching and learning in community. The second step invites the learner to engage with the topic or focus of the session, and the third step encourages individual and group responses to experiences of relating to the issues being discussed. If group members are reading the book together, giving brief assignments for reading and reflection enables their active participation and leadership in the session.

Each chapter in the book makes reference to a psalm. These psalms can be used to end each session meditatively. In a Benedictine form, psalms are read slowly without explanation, allowing room for silence. Another ancient way of meditation on God's Word is *lectio divina*, or "divine reading." Read the psalm three times. The first time ask individuals to listen for one word that they think describes what the psalm is saying. For the second reading, ask them to think of a phrase that summarizes the meaning of the psalm. For the third reading, invite them to respond with what they hear God asking them to do. Be sure to allow time for silence and meditation between each reading. This way of reading biblical text is suggested for use with youth in the Lutheran Bible Resource, *M Louie* (Augsburg Fortress, 2001). The prayers at the end of each session are all written by youth and are included in the book *Blessing New Voices: Prayers of Young People and Worship Resources for Youth Ministry* by Maren C. Tirabassi (Cleveland: United Church Press, 2000).

For a Six-Week Study

Preparation: Order copies of the books for the participants. Think about where the group will meet and the kind of seating arrangement that will enable conversation. Will you be seated around tables or more informally in a room with comfortable chairs? Consider having a worship center in the room with a cloth on a small table and a candle to light during the reading of the psalm and the prayer at the end of each session. Symbols representing the theme of each chapter could also be placed on the table: Session 1—objects connected with teenagers—like a T-shirt, backpack, and so on; Session 2—pictures of teenagers; Session 3— a plant and/or a package of seeds; Session 4—loaf of bread; Session 5—Bible; and Session 6—a backpack.

Session 1: Living In-Between

Gathering—5–10 minutes

The way you begin depends on the nature of the group. If people do not know each other, provide name tags. Have paper, markers, and crayons available. Ask the participants either to draw a symbol that represents a teenager they know or to write down five adjectives to describe this teenager.

Exploring—10 minutes

Invite people to introduce themselves (if the group members don't know one another) and to share their words or images. Discuss the class and the topics of discussion for each week and introduce this book to them.

Connecting—30

View the video *What's God Like?* from
youth and use the included leader's gu
see the resource section at the end of

Going—5–1

Give a preview of the next session a...
Living In-Between. Ask them to bring pictures o... ...
them. Discuss the issue of confidentiality and ask everyone to hono...
commitment that whatever is said in the room, stays in the room. Close
with a reading of Psalm 23 using either a Benedictine or *lectio divina*
way of reading and a prayer. Here is a prayer written by Craig Stevens:

> *Dear God, you are beyond the wind and in the clouds.*
>
> *Please also be in the shadows by our side, listening,*
>
> *When we need you. Amen.*

Session 2

Focus on discussion of Chapter 1, "Living In-Between," which consid-
ers who teenagers are from a developmental perspective.

Gathering—5 minutes

Collect the pictures parents have brought and have them on the table.
Collect pictures of all kinds of teenagers (ages thirteen to nineteen) from
newspapers and magazines and have them on the table as well. As people
arrive, invite them to look at the pictures noticing similarities and differences.

Exploring—30 minutes

These questions will facilitate discussion of this chapter. Choose from
among them to fit your group and its interests.

dyads, respond to this question: What are the memories you have of your own adolescence? It was a of . . . What is different for youth going through adolescence today in contrast to when you experienced it?"

On page 15 myths and realities of adolescence are discussed, what would you add to this list?

3. Refer to page 23 and this statement: "Essential for a teenager is the image of a bridge that, if it is to support the healthy transformation of an adolescent, must be firmly anchored on both ends as she or he moves between childhood and becoming a young adult." That paragraph then goes on to quote Robert Kegan who says. "People grow best where they continuously experience an ingenious blend of support and challenge." What have you found to be important in building this bridge of support and challenge?

4. What in the material in this chapter on development was new or thought provoking?

Connecting—15 minutes

Using Appendix 1, which provides a list of healthy identity characteristics of adolescents from Charles M. Shelton's book *Pastoral Counseling with Youth and Youth Adults*, engage the group in discussion of these questions:

1. Discuss each characteristic: Which of these characteristics are you seeing in your teenager? Which are fully present and which are beginning to emerge? Which are not yet visible?

2. Can you give some examples of how a teenager you know is growing into one of these characteristics?

3. What are the greatest challenges you have experienced in supporting your child as she or he moves from childhood into adolescence?

Going—5-10 minutes

Looking Ahead—Read chapter 2, "A Faith That Grows" for the next session. The focus for the next session is on youth and faith. In preparation for the discussion, pass out index cards and ask everyone to write down his or her questions of faith, questions about God, the Bible, and life. Ask them to bring the index cards back with them. No names need to be identified on the cards.

Close with a reading of Psalm 46 and a prayer of your own or this one written by Matt Loos.

> God, you have always been there for me in times when I needed help or guidance. You have given me many gifts of love, kindness, and faith. I know others will get just the same gifts. So keep me and my family and friends safe. But also keep the hungry fed, and get the poor money, and give the insecure people security and faith. Amen.

Session 3: A Faith That Grows

Gathering

As people gather, have a basket available on a table and ask them to put their index cards in the basket. For those who forgot or were not present for the last session, have cards available for them to write their questions of faith. Ask the participants to sit together in twos or threes and begin sharing their responses to these questions:

- What religious practices were part of your home when you were a child?

- Which, if any, of these do you continue now in your home? Any new practices?

Exploring

There are several quotes from Craig Dykstra's book, *Growing in the Life of Faith: Education and Christian Practices* included in this chapter. In the quote included here, he raises questions about how or if we use religious language. Use this quote for discussion with your group. Have it printed either on a handout or visible in the room:

Could it be that we do not know our faith's language because we simply do not live the form of life out of which such language grows? Perhaps our form of life is, in reality, so fully governed by another language that religious language is simply quaint and irrelevant . . . we do in fact hunger for this language. . . . The appropriation of a language does not happen just from hearing it. It happens through understanding it and speaking it. . . . The way of living deepens the understanding of the language, while a deepening understanding of the language enables new levels of participation in the way of living. Language and action cannot be separated.[1]

1. What religious language is part of your vocabulary?
2. What words used in worship are familiar to you? Which ones are more unfamiliar? What theological terms are familiar to you? Which ones are not? (Revelation, sin, judgment, redemption, providence, forgiveness, confession, assurance of pardon, and so on)
3. What examples can you think of from the life of your children and family that involved helping them connect their faith and their actions with theological language?

Connecting

Put the index cards of adult questions on a table, or tape them to a piece of newsprint. Have these questions of youth printed on newsprint. Invite the group to get up and wander around reading and reflecting on the questions of faith.

• What difference does it make . . .

To belong to a church?

How we interpret the Bible?

To be Presbyterian, Methodist, Baptist, United Church of Christ, Pentecostal, Catholic, Jewish, or Muslim?

To believe in God?

To be a Christian?

- Why, in the times of our ancestors, did God punish and speak to people so abundantly, while, in the present age, God rarely, if ever does the same?

- Why can't the Middle East live in peace?

- Why are some lives and places to live better than others?

- Why are only some of my prayers answered?

- In old times, God was the primary subject. Now God is not regarded as much as a primary subject or source. Why is this?

- Why in past times did God keep people who did good, like Moses or Paul, from harm, while in the present he lets people like Martin Luther King Jr. and John F. Kennedy be assassinated and hurt while they tried to do good.

- Why isn't God doing the same miracles today as in Jesus' time, such as talking directly to us? I know God is doing miracles in a different way today, not the direct approach. I would like it done both ways.

Questions for Discussion

1. What are the connections between questions of faith of youth and your questions?

2. Look together at the practices of faith described on page 41. Which of these are most essential in your own life of faith, in the life of your teenager, and in the life of your family?

3. Discuss responses to the questions on page 43 in the section of Chapter 2 entitled "Nurturing a Growing Faith."

Going

Ask the group to read the following pages of chapter three, "Good-Enough Parents." Read Psalm 27 and close with a prayer or this litany written by a youth church school class at St. Paul's Church in Lancaster, New Hampshire:

> *God, give us courage to grow up responsibly.*
>
> > *God, hear our prayer.*
>
> *God, give us gratitude for all your teachings.*
>
> > *God, hear our prayer.*
>
> *God, we give thanks for our families and the lessons they teach us.*
>
> > *God, hear our prayer.*
>
> *God, we give thanks for friends; help us to be good friends.*
>
> > *God, hear our prayer.*
>
> *God, let us make the right decision when we feel pressured.*
>
> > *God, hear our prayer.*
>
> *God, let us use our creativity and energy to help others.*
>
> > *God, hear our prayer.*

Session 4: "Good-Enough Parents"

This chapter is a bit different from the others in that it includes teaching and learning suggestions for five different educational opportunities. Read through these designs and select the parts you would like to use in this session, or you could follow the suggestions below.

Gathering

Use Appendix 3 "My Family" as a way to gather around the topic. You could reproduce the appendix page from the book or have the open-ended sentences printed on newsprint with markers available. Ask the participants to write their responses to the open-ended statements.

Exploring

1. What are some of the greatest challenges and blessings of being the parent of an adolescent?

2. Appendix 4, "Survival Skills for Parents and Teenagers," includes some information from a book by Michael Riera. Use this handout for discussion.

3. Discuss your response to the question asked on page 54, "When I think about being the parent of an adolescent, these are the most important things to remember."

Connecting

1. What are some ways your family protects its time together?

2. What places are important in the life of your family? How often do you visit them?

3. What interests does your family have in common?

4. What celebrations are important to your family? Which ones have you created?

Going

Chapter 4 is the reading for the next session. Close with a reading of Psalm 78 and this prayer written by Jeff Fahrenholz:

> Dear God, every day I am constantly reminded of your love. It comes in the form of my parents. I constantly test their love for me with my various actions. There are times when I feel as though I should actually lose their love, but I don't. And some days they get so mad at me and vice versa that I am sure my stable family relationships will shake apart. But every day, God, they forgive me and I forgive them. No matter what happens, I can feel their love. Their love shows itself to me in all the little things. I thank you for that love—it is your greatest gift to me. Amen.

Session 5: Teaching and Learning with Adolescents

Gathering

Invite the participants to share their responses to the following questions:

1. What do you remember of your confirmation experience or the time when you were welcomed into the membership of a congregation?

2. As you think about the continuing religious education of your teenager, what are your hopes? What do you hope they will learn and know? What experiences of the Christian faith do you want them to have?

Exploring

Discuss how would you respond to these open-ended sentences:

Confirmation is . . .

Confirmation is not . . .

Then look at Appendix 6, "What Confirmation Is, What It Is Not," and discuss the definitions that are included there and compare them with the participants' responses.

Connecting

The thesis of this chapter is that the congregation is an important partner with parents in nurturing the spiritual life of adolescents. Parents who participate with their teenagers in all the activities of a faithful congregation model for their child what church membership means. On page 75 of this chapter, in the section "What Precedes and What Follows in Religious Education," three questions are listed. Discuss these as a group.

Additional questions for discussion are these:

1. What is your church doing with youth or parents that really makes a difference in their lives?

2. What do youth need from their parents, family, and the church?

3. What do parents of teenagers most need from the church?

4. Youth ministry is . . .

Going

The reading for the last session is chapter 5, "A Backpack of Belonging." Ask for a volunteer to select a psalm of her or his choice with which to close the last session. Close with a reading of Psalm 65. Here is a prayer written by Joanna Begin.

> God, as you know, I'm not a saint, but with your help, I'm far from ordinary. I have learned so much from you and every day you gently guide me, teach me . . . and even when I stray from the path, I know you'll be there to set me straight. God, I just hope that your love for everyone can help me remember that, no matter what happens, I will stay calm, not prejudge. When I follow my heart, I find you. Thank you for everything you give me every day. I love you, God, more and more each day. Amen.

Session 6: A Backpack of Belonging

Gathering

As people arrive, give them a small index card or die-cut shapes (from a craft store or school supply) like a butterfly, cross, or handprint. Ask them to write on it something they would want their teenager to remember, something they could carry in their "backpack of belonging"—to a family and with a family of faith.

Exploring

Discuss the two major parts of this chapter, "Ten Things Youth Need," and then reflect on the list for parents (pages 106–107) What would you add to this last list?

Connecting

Invite people to share what they wrote in the gathering exercise and to come forward and place it in the backpack.

Going

Spend some time in intercessory prayer, and then close with either the psalm selected for this last session or Psalm 121. Here is a prayer written by Kristi Orr:

> Dear God, please help me be strong while I go through a difficult part of my life. Please help me make the right decisions as I live my life. I know I will be facing a lot of problems in my teenage years. Life is very difficult, and I will look to you to help me. I know I will make my own decisions, but I will look toward you for advice. I am constantly reminded of your love and care. Amen.

For a Four-Week Study

Use the same process of teaching and learning as with the six-week study. Select the focus for the four sessions based on interest and priorities for the small group or follow this suggestion.

Session 1—Living In-Between

Session 2—Good-Enough Parents

Session 3—A Faith That Grows

Session 4—A Backpack of Belonging

Resources for Use with Adolescents, Parents, and Teachers

Books on Adolescents

Bradley, Michael J. *Yes, Your Teen Is Crazy! Loving Your Kid without Losing Your Mind.* Gig Harbor, Wash.: Harbor Press, 2002.

Brown, Lyn Mikel and Carol Gilligan. *Meeting at the Crossroads: Women's Psychology and Girls' Development.* Cambridge, Mass.: Harvard University Press, 1992.

Cohen-Sandler, Roni. *Trust Me, Mom—Everyone Else Is Going: The New Rules for Mothering Adolescent Girls.* New York: Viking Press, 2002.

Davis, Patricia H. *Counseling Adolescent Girls.* Minneapolis: Augsburg/Fortress, 1996.

Elkind, David. *All Grown Up and No Place to Go.* Reading, Mass.: Addison-Wesley, 1998.

Hersch, Patricia. *A Tribe Apart: A Journey Into the Heart of American Adolescence.* New York: Ballantine, 1998.

Lesko, Nancy. *Act Your Age! A Cultural Construction of Adolescence.* New York: Routledge Falmer, 2001.

Ms. Foundation for Women and Sondra Forsyth. *Girls Seen and Heard: 52 Life Lessons for Our Daughters.* New York: Jeremy P. Tarcher/Putnam, 1998.

Ng, David, ed., *People on the Way: Asian North Americans Discovering Christ, Culture, and Community.* Valley Forge, Pa.: Judson Press, 1996.

Orenstein, Peggy. *Schoolgirls: Young Women, Self-Esteem, and the Confidence Gap.* New York: Anchor Books, 1994.

Pipher, Mary. *Reviving Ophelia: Saving the Selves of Adolescent Girls.* New York: Ballantine Books, 1994.

Pollack, William. *Real Boys: Rescuing Our Sons from the Myths of Boyhood.* New York: Henry Holt & Company, 1998.

Riera, Michael. *Uncommon Sense for Parents with Teenagers.* Berkeley, Calif.: Celestial Arts, 1995.

Riera, Michael and Joseph De Prisco. *Field Guide to the American Teenager: A Parent's Companion.* Cambridge, Mass.: Perseus Publishing, 2000.

Roehlkepartain, Eugene C. and Dorothy L. Williams. *Exploring Faith Maturity: A Self-Study Guide for Teenagers.* Minneapolis: Search Institute, 1990.

Rowatt, G. Wade, Jr. *Adolescents in Crisis: A Guide for Parents, Teachers, Ministers, and Counselors.* Louisville: Westminster John Knox Press, 2001.

Shelton, Charles. *Pastoral Counseling with Adolescents and Young Adults.* New York: Crossroad Publishing, 1995.

Taffel, Ron. *The Second Family: How Adolescent Power Is Challenging the American Family.* New York: St. Martin's Press, 2001.

Videos

The best source for video rental is Travarca, an audiovisual library of the Reformed Church in America and the Christian Reformed Church in North America. Their toll-free number is 800-968-7221, e-mail is travarca@iserv.net. Yearly memberships for congregations are available and provide unlimited video rental. Individual videos can be rented by nonmembers as well. Their video catalog is updated yearly.

Ecufilm is an ecumenical source for videos for purchase.

Help! My Teenager Is Driving Me Crazy—28-minute video that explores issues of parenting teenagers. Part of a series, "Survival Guide for Adults."

Videos helpful in teaching and learning with youth are:

What's God Like?—20-minute video from the Questions of Faith for Youth series.

How Do You Spell God?—32-minute video based on the book by Rabbi Marc Gellman and Monsignor Thomas Hartman.

What's the Holy Spirit?—25-minute video from the Questions of Faith Series for Adults.

How to Get Blessed without Sneezing: Rediscovering the Beatitudes—28 minutes of humorous scenes with two actors representing the truths of the beatitudes.

The Growing Edge: Youth Encounters in Worship—20-minute video of teenagers participating in worship in diverse settings and then reflecting on their experiences.

Parables That Jesus Told—30-minute video narrated by Garrison Keilor that explores the meaning of the parables of the sower and the prodigal son.

For Parents, Pastors, Educators, Teachers, and Leaders of Youth

Dean, Kenda Creasy and Ron Foster. *The Godbearing Life: The Art of Soul Tending for Youth Ministry.* Nashville: Upper Room Books, 1998.

Gardner, Howard. *Intelligence Reframed: Multiple Intelligences for the 21st Century.* New York: Basic Books, 1999.

Gee, Martha Bettis. *Things to Make and Do for Advent and Christmas; Things to Make and Do for Lent and Easter; Things to Make and Do for Pentecost; Things to Make and Do Anytime.* Louisville: Bridge Resources, 1998. Although written for use in ministry with children, many of the art activities are also appropriate for use with youth.

Harris, Maria. *Fashion Me a People: Curriculum in the Church.* Louisville: Westminster/John Knox Press, 1989.

MacQueen, Neil and Melissa Armstrong-Hansche. *Workshop Rotation: A New Model for Sunday School.* Louisville: Geneva Press, 2000.

Nishioka, Rodger. *Rooted in Love: 52 Meditations and Stories for Youth Ministry Leaders.* Louisville: Bridge Resources, 1997.

Norris, Kathleen. *Cloister Walk.* New York: Riverhead Books, 1996.

————. *Dakota.* New York: Tichnor & Fields, 1993.

————. *Amazing Grace: A Vocabulary of Faith.* New York: Riverhead Books, 1998.

Roehlkepartian, Eugene. *Growing Up Generous: Engaging Youth In Living and Serving.* Washington, D.C.: Alban Institute, 2000.

Books to Use with Youth

Bass, Dorothy C. and Don C. Richter, eds. *Way to Live: Christian Practices for Teens.* Nashville: Upper Room Books, 2002.

Tirabassi, Maren C. *Blessing New Voices: Prayers of Young People and Worship Resources for Youth Ministry.* Cleveland: United Church Press, 2000.

Two publications from the Upper Room are available for youth. *Devo 'Zine* is a devotional magazine written for youth. *Alive Now* is appropriate for youth and parents.

Books to Use with Parents/Adults in Discussion Groups

Alperson, Myra. *Dim Sum, Bagels, and Grits: A Sourcebook for Multicultural Families.* New York: Farrar, Straus and Giroux, 2001.

Bass, Dorothy. *Practicing Our Faith: A Way of Life for a Searching People.* San Francisco: Jossey-Bass, 1997.

Dykstra, Craig. *Growing in the Life of Faith: Education and Christian Practices.* Louisville: Westminster/John Knox Press, 1999.

Kegan, Robert. *In over Our heads: The Mental Demands of Modern Life.* Cambridge: Harvard University Press, 1994.

Peterson, Eugene H. *Like Dew Your Youth: Growing Up with Your Teenager.* Grand Rapids, Mich.: Eerdmans, 1976.

Pipher, Mary. *The Shelter of Each Other: Rebuilding Our Families.* Grossett/Putnam, 1996.

Stinnett, Nick and John DeFrain. *Secrets of Strong Families*. New York: Berkley Books, 1985.

Wuthnow, Robert. *Growing Up Religious: Christians and Jews and Their Journeys of Faith*. Boston: Beacon Press, 1999.

Web sites

Here's a list of Web sites I find helpful in thinking about youth and faith:

Alternatives for Simple Living—alternatives.org offers helpful resources

American Bible Society—abs.com

Parenting for Peace and Justice—ppj.org

practicingourfaith.org—information about Christian practices and resources for living the Christian faith. Look at the Youth Connections part of the Web site.

sundaysoftware.com—site of a Presbyterian minister, Neil MacQueen. Offers information on computer programs and technology for resources for Christian education.

rotation.org—information on a rotation model of church school and links to rotation model curriculum. (See chapter 4 about this model.)

search-institute.org—a resource for ministry with youth with a particular focus on building assets.

Curriculum Resources

Willimon, William H. *Making Disciples*. Logos Productions, 1997. (800-328-0200) This confirmation curriculum is designed to be taught in a one-on-one adult youth model. It is unique in not following a traditional classroom model.

Myers, William R., ed. *Becoming and Belonging: A Practical Design for Confirmation*. Cleveland: United Church Press, 1993. This book offers planning help for those interested in designing their own confirmation curriculum.

Browning, Robert L. and Roy A. Reed. *Models of Confirmation and Baptismal Affirmation: Liturgical and Educational Issues and Designs*. Birmingham: Religious Education Press, 1995. For those interested in the history and traditions of confirmation education, this is for you!

Claim the Name is the confirmation curriculum of the United Methodist Church. Resources available include Confirmation Teaching plans for groups that meet from six to fifteen weeks and groups that meet for thirty-nine weeks. Other resources are *TalkPoints, Faith Exploration for Older Youth and Adults,* and twelve retreat designs to use with younger and older youth. Contact cokesbury.com.

Journeys in Faith: A Guide for Confirmation/Commissioning is the confirmation curriculum of the Presbyterian Church (U.S.A.).

Affirming Faith: A Congregation's Guide to Confirmation is the confirmation curriculum of the United Church of Christ.

The Evangelical Lutheran Church of America (ELCA) offers a variety of confirmation resources—*Creative Confirmation, Living in Grace,* and *To Know, to Live, to Grow.*
     Two separate pieces of curriculum that could be adapted for use by non-Lutherans are *What Is This? Faith Conversations for Mentors and Youth* and *What Is This? Faith Conversations for Parents and Youth.* All ELCA resources are available at www.augsburgfortress.org.

Post-Confirmation Curriculum

Visit denominational Web sites and check the links to curriculum for youth. Two newer curriculum worth considering are:

Firelight—curriculum produced by Lutherans (ELCA) for the workshop rotation model. Titles available are: *God Feeds Us; God Comes to Us; Surprised by God's Grace; Come to God's Party!; Let's Practice Faith;* and *Peace Be with You.* Available from Augsburg Fortress, 800-328-4678 or their Web site.

Seasons of the Spirit is a new (Fall 2002) lectionary-based curriculum from the joint efforts of the United Church of Canada and the United Church of Christ. It is available through the United Church Press (800-537-3394), United Methodist Publishing House (800-672-1789), or Logos Productions (800-328-0200). Visit the Web site at www.spiritseasons.com.

Appendices

Appendix 1
Adolescents and Identity Changes

In his book *Pastoral Counseling with Adolescents and Young Adults*, Charles M. Shelton has identified a list of identity characteristics. He believes that adults can use these as a checklist as they think about the identity formation of teenagers.

1. Growing time perspective—Teenagers understand time in all of its movements from past to present and to future.

2. Finding time for solitude—As adolescents mature, they are capable of spending time alone.

3. Inner complexity—Shelton sees three dimensions of a young person's identity formation. As teenagers mature, they are able to: think more deeply about complex issues; tolerate ambivalence in relationships; and be self-reflective.

4. Growing boundaries—As they mature, adolescents know appropriate boundaries within the family, in interpersonal relationships, and with peers.

5. Development of healthy relationships—Are the relationships of a teenager marked by trust, honesty, the values held dear by the family?

6. Growing self-acceptance—The acceptance of physical changes.

7. Knowledge of roles—A teenager's ability to both understand and balance the various roles in her or his life.

8. Develop a philosophy of life—The evidence of being able to articulate personal views of life.

9. Competency functioning—The signs of confidence and competence in handling life's opportunities and challenges.

10. Appropriate display of emotion—The ability to control and be aware of one's emotions and the appropriateness of one's expression.[1]

Appendix 2
Parenting Principles

Ten Principles of Parenting:
Evelyn Lee

1. Understand your teenager's physical and psychological needs.
2. Improve communication.
3. Use appropriate rewards and discipline.
4. Encourage initiative and independence.
5. Provide guidance in your teenager's life.
6. Encourage extracurricular activities.
7. Know your teenager's school environment.
8. Develop a positive cultural identity.
9. Maintain family harmony.
10. Utilize community resources.[2]

Ten Commandments of Parenting:
Michael J. Bradley

1. Thou shalt be as the dispassionate copy unto thine Own child: be cool, not the fool.
2. Thou shalt listen as thine own child shouts.
3. Thou shalt not shout: speak thou wisely.
4. Thou shalt add fifteen minutes to every interaction involving thy teen.
5. Thou shalt vanquish thy foolish pride.
6. Thou shalt not kill.
7. Thou shalt apologize at every opportunity.
8. Thou shalt honor thy child's identity (even though it maketh you ill).
9. To thine own self be true.
10. Know Thou, this too shall pass.[3]

Qualities of Strong Families:
Nick Stinnett and John DeFrain

Commitment
Time
Appreciation

Communication
Coping Ability
Spiritual wellness [4]

Traits of Healthy Families:
Dolores Curran

1. Communicates and listens.
2. Affirms and supports one another.
3. Teaches respect for one another.
4. Develops a sense of trust.
5. Has a sense of play and humor.
6. Exhibits a sense of shared responsibility.
7. Teaches a sense of right and wrong.
8. Has a strong sense of family—honors rituals and traditions.
9. Has a balance of interaction among members.
10. Has a shared religious core.
11. Respects each other's privacy.
12. Values service to others.
13. Foster family table time and conversation.
14. Shares leisure time.
15. Admits to/seeks help with problems. [5]

Appendix 3
My Family

My family is like a . . . because . . .
We are a good family because we . . .

Good families are about joy. Strong families find ways to make time sacred, to make days special. People eat, sing, and play together. They make jokes and hug, smile at the thought of a get-together. Strong families find something to appreciate in every day and teach their members to wrest beauty from a mottled reality. [6]

Strong families are "places where we enter for comfort, development, and regeneration and places from which we go forth renewed and charged with power for positive living." [7]

Appendix 4
Survival Skills for Parents and Teenagers

Adolescence is not a phase of life to be feared; rather, it is one of fascination, curiosity, and unexpected twists, and as such, it is quite different from the previous stages of childhood. What parents need is a translation of this period that makes sense and is useful.[8]

- What changes in your child have you begun to notice as they move into adolescence?
- Michael Riera says that teenagers experience change in these areas: physical and cognitive; social; friendship; personal identity; and family and life events. In what ways have these changes been a challenge for you as a parent?
- What do you remember from your own adolescence?
- How would you describe your role as a parent with your teenage daughter or son? What does your teenager need from you now that is different from when she or he was a child? What is consistent in your parenting?
- Michael Riera suggests that often parents act as managers in their child's life. You make all the arrangements for their life and are closely informed about all aspects of their life at home and at school. Then the change happens and Riera says that you are fired as manager. "Now you must scramble and restrategize; if you are to have meaningful influence in your teenager's life through adolescence and beyond, then you must work your tail off to get rehired as consultant."[9]
  In what ways do you agree or disagree with Riera's statement? Are there other terms you would use to describe your role as parent with your teenager?

Appendix 5
Suggestions for Mentors

1. Read the books by William Willimon on mentoring. This curriculum was designed to be used as confirmation curriculum in a mentoring (one-on-one) model of education. Use it as a resource in any way you think best.

2. Spend some time getting to know each other. You might also speak to a parent of the youth for whom you are a mentor and introduce yourself if you don't know her or him.

3. Exchange phone numbers or e-mail addresses.

4. Find a time to meet, at least once a month from now through May.

5. Volunteer to do something together at church.

6. Mentoring is another way that youth learn about the Christian faith and why it is important to adults. Consider mentoring as a spiritual practice. Keep this teenager and her or his family in your prayers.

A guarantor is like a living wilderness marker, one who stands as an adult but who also helpfully walks with a youth on his or her journey. Guarantors share the burden of the journey, help read the road maps, raise the hard questions of faith, and offer needed encouragement. They incarnate "adultness" in ways that encourage young people to grow. They embody the faith in a variety of forms. In this way, they "guarantee" the good news that adulthood is feasible and that the Christian story is also their story.[10]

Appendix 6
What Confirmation Is, What It Is Not

Every year we "take in new members" and young people "join." But we don't reflect often on the fact that joining means belonging to and belonging with and belonging for. . . . In most of the ways we structure it, church membership is incidental—sort of an extra that we do like deciding where to shop or where to bank or where to go to college for awhile. . . . Church membership is joining a story, joining a vision, joining a crunch.[11]

WALTER BRUGGEMANN

The church that recognizes the tension existing between the expectations of our culture and the covenantal significance of baptism can begin to understand confirmation as a rite that confirms a personal acceptance by the confirmand of baptismal vows, carrying an accompanying increase in the ministerial responsibilities of new community members, and affirming—in real ways—the vocation of both its adolescent and adult believers. Viewed in this fourfold fashion, the covenantal faithfulness of a church is suspect to the degree that it fails to accept and integrate into the congregation those adolescents and adults who complete such a faithful process.[12]

WILLIAM MYERS

Confirmation as blessing by God, the faith community, and the family should have a relational quality which is empowering and substantial. . . . The great sacramental experiences of baptism, confirmation, and eucharist then become the primary paradigms for blessing children, youth, and adults and giving them a vision of their meaning, purpose, and eternal destiny in life's pilgrimage.[13]

ROBERT BROWNING AND ROY REED

Two qualities of special importance in companioning a teen adult are a life of public and private prayer and a life of commitment to community building and peacemaking. These qualities comprise "Adult Christianity 101." Without them, Christianity is merely a game. With them, the journey has a beginning, a direction, and a goal. It is a journey of faith, ongoing conversion, with Christ as the beginning and end.[14]

JAMES WILDE

Confirmation is the opportunity a congregation has to bless the growth in faith of its youth. In the act of confirming faith, a youth is publicly commissioned for mission and ministry as a faithful Christian in their congregation, their community, and in the world. It also offers the opportunity for adults to be involved in the lives of its adolescents as teachers, mentors, and friends. Welcoming adolescents into membership and commissioning them for faithful ministry in the church and in the world is an act of faith and hope.

Appendix 7
Confirmation Projects

You will have three weeks to work on a confirmation project—March 10, 17, and 24. Easter Sunday is March 31 and there will be no church school. We can all go to the Easter breakfast. For your project, you can work alone or with a partner.

Select the project or projects from the list below. If we are discovering that more time is needed to complete the projects, we can also use some Sunday morning time in April. We will share your work on these projects when we meet with the Session in May the Monday before you are confirmed, May 19 (Pentecost Sunday). Circle the project or projects you want to work on and write your name at the bottom and give this to your teachers.

PROJECT TYPES

Interviews and Research
Art
Computers (Only two can work on internal projects each week.)
Music
Inside/Outside

ONE-WEEK PROJECTS

1. Interview our mission volunteers, and find out what they have been doing this year.
2. Compare and contrast two children's Bible storybooks—what Old Testament stories are included, omitted? What stories about Jesus and the church are included? Which stories are illustrated? (Recall the kinds of writings in the Bible.)
3. Read the Gospel of Matthew. Using a Bible atlas, draw a map showing the places Jesus traveled.
4. Using clay, create a visual image of one of your favorite Bible stories or verses. (This could continue over two to three weeks.)
5. Using your Bible and the art books, find paintings that you think best illustrate stories or ideas from the Bible.
6. Using paints and stamping, make a table runner to use on Wednesday nights—symbols could represent seasons of the church year. (This could continue over two to three weeks.)
7. Some people like to use prayer beads for their personal time of meditation or prayer. (Like the WWJD chain you made for the kids.) Make some prayer beads to give as a Lenten gift to members in the church who are sick, or to leave on the pillow of our Room in the Inn guests.
8. Visit the Web site for the Presbyterian Church—pcusa.org. Find ten facts about the church that are new to you.
9. Visit one of the following Web sites. What resources do they have? What is their Web site communicating about the Christian faith?
- American Bible Society—abs.com
- Alternatives for Simple Living—alternatives.org

- Parenting for Peace and Justice——ppj.org

10. Learn something about another faith tradition—visit Web sites of other churches and find out what they believe.

11. Spend some time with the Presbyterian Hymnbook. What do our hymns reveal about what we believe about God, the Spirit, Jesus, the church?

12. Work on helping clean up trash, and so on around the church.

13. Help teach in the preschool. (This could be more than one week.)

14. Volunteer to help cook or serve the meal or to help with the setup for the sunrise service and breakfast or for the Easter breakfast at church.

Two–Three Week Projects

15. Interview five to ten people older than you with one of these questions or another of your choice: What is your biggest question about God, faith, and life? What is your favorite Bible verse or story? Why?

16. Find two to three people who were members of a church other than Presbyterian before joining Second Presbyterian. Find out why they joined Second.

17. Think about a couple of older members of the congregation. Call them and ask if you can interview them during church school to learn some of the history of our church.

18. Using available resource books, think about the meaning of Pentecost and images used in representing it. Make a banner to use in worship on Pentecost/Confirmation Sunday.

19. Using a video camera, make a brief movie, "A Sunday in the Life of Second Presbyterian."

20. Try your hand at batik and make a cloth for the communion table.

21. After reading through some of the Gospel of Matthew, illustrate with collage or watercolors, the scenes in the life of Jesus that you think are most significant.

22. Use a camera and take pictures of all kinds of people and activities at church to make an album "Faces and Places of Second."

23. Take pictures of each member of the confirmation class and include a short biography.

24. Create a PowerPoint presentation that tells the story of this confirmation class and what we have been learning together.

25. Think about the music we could use on Pentecost Sunday. Plan what we will sing. Is there someone interested in playing an instrument?

26. Interview one or two of the musicians in our congregation and find out about how they go about writing music to use in worship.
27. Make a light board for use in the Peaceable Kingdom.
28. Work on the bulletin for Pentecost. Help in writing the call to worship or prayer of confession.

NAME _____
(If you chose a project that requires the use of a video camera or camera, please tell us if you have one at home that you can bring with you.)

Appendix 8
An Individualized Confirmation Education Program

Exploration in Faith is the name of the confirmation education program at Immanuel Presbyterian Church in Milwaukee, Wisconsin. The pastor, the Reverend Dr. Deborah Block, designed it for older youth in grades 11-12, and it is a good example of a model of teaching and learning that affirms individual and communal learning.

The nine-month program includes a service of commissioning in September when the youth who are participating sign a covenant indicating their commitment to participation and completion of the learning opportunities in the three areas of worship, study, and service. The class ends with their confirmation on Pentecost Sunday. The purpose of this educational experience is to confirm Christian faith and enable older youth to assume adult membership in the church. In this model, older youth work with their pastor in making decisions about how they will satisfy the unit requirements in worship, study, and service.

Each youth is expected to complete twelve units of worship, study, and service. (One unit is the equivalent of two hours.)

WORSHIP (12 units):
1 Sunday morning service = 1 unit
special services = 1 unit
(out of 37 Sundays and 24 special services)

STUDY (12 units):
6 units are completed by meeting together for "Second Sunday Suppers" and discussion on the following topics:

November—The Bible Is Your Story
December—The Meaning of Jesus
January—Making Disciples (Vocation)
February—Making Decisions (Vocation)
March—Why the Church?
April—Faith Matters
+ session(s) as needed to complete Statement of Faith

remaining units from
Saturday seminars (2 units)
Sunday morning adult education (1/2 unit)
Wednesday evening house church gatherings (Lent) (1 unit)
and

1 prospective member orientation evening
October, February, or May
1 congregational meeting
special or annual (January or May)
2 individual modules with minister ("confirmation conversations")

SERVICE (12 units):
(in consultation with Dr. Block)
sing in choir
assist in church school
summer mission trip
Food Pantry
usher on Sunday morning
UNICEF project for younger children
CROP Walk in October
Alternative Christmas market
work with One Great Hour of Sharing committee
Earth Day/Creation Sunday project (April)
Christmas trees and boughs
special projects

Notes

Chapter 1: Living In-Between

1. Joe Zefran qtd. in Sydney Lewis, *"A Totally Alien Life-Form"—Teenagers* (New York: The New Press, 1996), 83.

2. Mary Pipher, *Reviving Ophelia, Saving the Selves of Adolescent Girls* (New York: Ballantine, 1994), 52–53.

3. Lyn Mikel Brown and Carol Gilligan, *Meeting at the Crossroads: Women's Psychology and Girls' Development* (Cambridge: Harvard University Press, 1992), 217.

4. G. Wade Rowatt Jr., *Adolescents in Crisis: A Guide for Parents, Teachers, Ministers, and Counselors* (Louisville: Westminster John Knox Press, 2001), 17.

5. David Elkind, *All Grown Up and No Place to Go: Teenagers in Crisis* (Reading, Mass.: Addison-Wesley, 1998).

6. Pipher, *Reviving Ophelia*, 52.

7. Joan Scheff Lipsitz, "Adolescent Development, Myths, and Realities," *Children Today* (Sept.-Oct. 1979): 49–50.

8. Ibid., 50.

9. Pipher, *Reviving Ophelia*, 19.

10. Ibid., 43.

11. Brown and Gilligan, *Meeting at the Crossroads*, 6.

12. William Pollack, *Real Boys: Rescuing Our Sons from the Myths of Boyhood* (New York: Henry Holt & Company, 1998), xxv.

13. Ibid., 5.

14. Nancy Lesko, *Act Your Age! A Cultural Construction of Adolescence*, (New York: Routledge, 2001), 1.

15. Ibid., 130–31.

16. Rowatt, *Adolescents in Crisis,* 18.

17. Charles M. Shelton, *Pastoral Counseling with Adolescents and Young Adults* (New York: Crossroad, 1995), 35.

18. L.S. Vygotskii, *Mind in Society: The Development of Higher Psychological Processes* (Cambridge: Harvard University Press, 1978), 86–87.

19. Michael J. Bradley, *Yes, Your Teen Is Crazy! Loving Your Kid without Losing Your Mind* (Gig Harbor, Wash.: Harbor Press, 2002), 5.

20. Ibid., 7.

21. Robert Kegan, *In over Our Heads: The Mental Demands of Modern Life* (Cambridge: Harvard University Press, 1994), 43.

22. Ibid., 42.

23. Bernhard W. Anderson, *Out of the Depths: The Psalms Speak for Us Today* (Philadelphia: Westminster Press, 1983), 36.

24. Ibid., 195.

Chapter 2: A Faith That Grows

1. Kenda Creasy Dean and Ron Foster, *The Godbearing Life: The Art of Soul Tending for Youth Ministry* (Nashville: Upper Room, 1998), 65.

2. Kathleen Norris, *Cloister Walk* (New York: Riverhead, 1996), 90–91.

3. Robert Wuthnow, *Growing Up Religious: Christians and Jews and Their Journeys of Faith* (Boston: Beacon, 1999), xxxvii–xxxviii.

4. Wuthnow, *Growing Up Religious,* xxxvii.

5. Kathleen Norris, *Dakota: A Spiritual Geography* (New York: Tichnor & Fields, 1993), 2.

6. Craig Dykstra, *Growing in the Life of Faith: Education and Christian Practices* (Louisville: Westminster John Knox Press, 1999), 121.

7. James Fowler, "The Public Church: Ecology for Faith Education and Advocate for Children," *Faith Development in Early Childhood,* ed. Doris Blazer (Kansas City, Mo.: Sheed and Ward, 1989), 141.

8. Ibid.

9. These faith styles are described in John H. Westerhoff, *Will Our Children Have Faith?* (Harrisburg, Pa.: Morehouse, 2000).

10. Robert Kegan, *The Evolving Self* (Cambridge: Harvard University Press, 1982), 121.

11. Walter Brueggemann, *The Message of the Psalms* (Minneapolis: Augsburg, 1984), 19.

12. Cited in Charles M. Shelton, *Pastoral Counseling with Adolescents and Young Adults* (New York: Crossroad, 1995), 47.

13. Eugene C. Roehlkepartain and Dorothy L. Williams, *Exploring Faith Maturity: A Self-Study Guide for Teenagers* (Minneapolis: Search Institute, 1990).

14. Wuthnow, *Growing Up Religious,* xxvi, xxxii, xxxvi.

15. Dorothy Bass, *Practicing Our Faith: A Way of Life for a Searching People* (San Francisco: Jossey-Bass, 1997), xi.

16. Dykstra, *Growing in the Life of Faith,* 43.

17. Ibid.

18. Ibid., 124.

19. Ibid.

20. For more information on the form of lament psalms, see Bernhard W. Anderson, *Out of the Depths: The Psalms Speak for Us Today.*

21. Ibid., 76.

22. Ann Weems, *Psalms of Lament* (Louisville: Westminster/John Knox, 1995), 73.

Chapter 3: Good-Enough Parents

1. Michael J. Bradley, *Yes, Your Teen Is Crazy! Loving Your Kid without Losing Your Mind* (Gig Harbor, Wash.: Harbor Press, 2002), 4.

2. Ibid., 19.

3. Amanda Cross, *Honest Doubt* (New York: Ballantine Books, 2000), 177.

4. William Myers, *Theological Themes in Youth Ministry* (Cleveland: Pilgrim Press, 1987), 30.

5. Ginny Munn, in Mary Motley Kalergis, *Seen and Heard: Teenagers Talk about Their Lives* (New York: Stewart, Tabori & Chang, 1998), 75.

6. Lily Wong, ibid., 119.

7. George Powell, ibid., 48.

8. Ramiro Rodriguez, in Sydney Lewis, *"A Totally Alien Life-Form"—Teenagers* (New York: The New Press, 1996), 137.

9. Sabrina Allen, ibid., 29.

10. Michael Riera, *Uncommon Sense for Parents with Teenagers* (Berkeley, Ca.: Celestial Arts, 1995), 11.

11. David Elkind, *All Grown Up and No Place to Go: Teenagers in Crisis* (Reading, Mass.: Addison-Wesley, 1998), 10.

12. Ibid., 13.

13. Grace Sangok Kim, "Asian North American Immigrant Parents and Youth: Parenting and Growing Up in a Cultural Gap," in *People on the Way: Asian North Americans Discovering Christ, Culture, and Community*, ed. David Ng (Valley Forge, Pa.: Judson Press, 1996),140.

14. Mary Pipher, *The Shelter of Each Other: Rebuilding Our Families* (New York: Grossett/Putnam, 1996), 23.

15. Ron Taffel, *The Second Family: How Adolescent Power Is Challenging the American Family* (New York: St. Martin's Press, 2001), 83.

16. Ibid., 80.

17. Ibid., 81.

18. G. Wade Rowatt, Jr., *Adolescents in Crisis: A Guide for Parents, Teachers, Ministers, and Counselors* (Louisville: Westminster John Knox Press, 2001), 8.

19. Ibid., 9.

20. Nick Stinnett and John DeFrain, *Secrets of Strong Families* (New York: Berkley Books, 1985), 8.

21. Ibid.

22. Bradley, *Yes, Your Teen Is Crazy!*, 180.

23. Bonnie Miller McLemore, *Also a Mother: Work and Family as Theological Dilemma* (Nashville: Abingdon Press, 1994), 186.

24. Janet Fishburn, *Confronting the Idolatry of Family: A New Vision for the Household of God* (Nashville: Abingdon Press, 1991), 141.

25. Riera, *Uncommon Sense for Parents with Teenagers,* 204.

26. Ibid., 206.

27. See Judith Viorst, *Alexander and the Terrible, Horrible, No Good, Very Bad Day* (New York: Atheneum, 1972).

28. Bernhard W. Anderson, *Out of the Depths: The Psalms Speak to Us Today* (Louisville: Westminster, 1983), 53.

29. Ibid., 55.

30. Ibid., 45.

Chapter 4: Confirmed and Commissioned: Connecting Faith and Life

1. Janet Fishburn, *Confronting the Idolatry of Family: A New Vision for the Household of God* (Nashville: Abingdon Press, 1991), 50.

2. William R. Myers, ed., *Becoming and Belonging: A Practical Design for Confirmation* (Cleveland: United Church Press, 1993), 9.

3. Walter Brueggemann, "Confirmation: Joining a Special Story," *Colloquy* (May/June 1974): 6–9.

4. Myers, ed., *Becoming and Belonging*, 13.

5. Robert L. Browning and Roy A. Reed, *Models of Confirmation and Baptismal Affirmation: Liturgical and Educational Issues and Designs* (Birmingham: Religious Education Press, 1995), 63, 66.

6. Gail Ramshaw, quoted in Kathleen Norris, *Cloister Walk* (New York: Riverhead Books, 1996), 61.

7. Norris, *Cloister Walk*, 64.

8. Thanks to the Reverend Mark Asleson of Dilworth Lutheran Church in Dilworth, Minnesota for sharing this story.

9. Maria Harris, *Fashion Me a People: Curriculum in the Church* (Louisville: Westminster/John Knox Press, 1989), 16.

10. For more information on this model of church education for children, visit these Web sites, rotation.org or sundaysoftware.com, or look at this book by Neil MacQueen and Melissa Armstrong-Hansche, *Workshop Rotation: A New Model for Sunday School* (Louisville: Geneva Press, 2000).

11. These five forms of curriculum are more fully described in Maria Harris, *Fashion Me a People: Curriculum in the Church* (Louisville: Westminster/John Knox Press, 1989).

12. Ibid., 63.

13. Kathleen Norris, *Amazing Grace: A Vocabulary of Faith* (New York: Riverhead Books, 1998), 2.

14. Howard Gardner, *Intelligence Reframed: Multiple Intelligences for the 21st Century* (New York: Basic Books, 1999), 204.

15. For further explanation of the eight intelligences, see Thomas Armstrong, *Multiple Intelligences in the Classroom*, 2d ed. (Alexandria, Va.: Association for Supervision and Curriculum Development, 2000).

16. For more information about these two curriculums, see pottersworkshop.org and cornerstones.org.

17. William Willimon, "Taking Confirmation out of the Classroom" in *Christian Century*, March 16, 1988, 271–271.

18. Ibid.

19. Ibid.

20. Ibid.

21. *The Faces of Jesus*, text by Frederick Buechner, photographs by Lee Boltin (Stearns/Harper and Row, 1989) and *Imaging the Word: Arts and Lectionary Resource*, vols. 1, 2, and 3, (Cleveland, Ohio: United Church Press).

22. William Myers, *Theological Themes in Youth Ministry* (Cleveland: Pilgrim Press, 1987), xviii.

23. Thanks to my friend Greg Bostrom for sharing this model of confirmation education used at Wildwood Presbyterian Church, Wildwood, Illinois.

24. William H. Willimon, *Making Disciples: Mentor's Guide* (Inner Grove Heights, Minn.: Logos Productions, 1997), 4.

25. Myers, *Becoming and Belonging*, 13.

26. Fishburn, *Confronting the Idolatry of Family*, 50.

27. Carol and Larry Nyberg, "Rekindling the Gift of God in Youth," in *Confirmed as Children, Affirmed as Teens* (Chicago: Liturgy Training Publications, 1990), 81.

28. Walter Brueggemann, *Praying the Psalms* (Winona, Minn.: Saint Mary's Press, 1993), 23.

Chapter 5: A Backpack of Belonging

1. Barbara Kimes Myers and William Myers, *Engaging in Transcendence: The Church's Ministry and Covenant with Young Children* (Cleveland, Ohio: United Church Press, 1992), 94.
2. Pipher, *The Shelter of Each Other,* 230.
3. Thanks to the Reverend Greg Bostrom for sharing this story.
4. Kent Haruf, *Plainsong* (New York: Alfred A. Knopf, 2000), 112.
5. Gail Godwin, *Evensong* (New York: Ballantine Books, 1999), 75–76.

Chapter 6: Suggestions for Teaching and Resources

1. Craig Dykstra, *Growing in the Life of Faith: Education and Christian Practices* (Louisville: Westminster/John Knox Press, 1999), 124–26.

Appendices

1. Charles M. Shelton, *Pastoral Counseling with Adolescents and Young Adults* (New York: Crossroad, 1995), 38–45.
2. Evelyn Lee, "Ten Principles on Raising Chinese American Teens," cited in "Asian North American Immigrant Parents and Youth: Parenting and Growing Up in a Cultural Gap" by Grace Sangok Kim in *People on the Way: Asian North Americans Discovering Christ, Culture, and Community,* ed. David Ng (Valley Forge, Pa., Judson Press, 1996), 144.
3. Michael J. Bradley, *Yes, Your Teen is Crazy! Loving Your Kid Without Losing Your Mind* (Gig Harbor, Wash.: Harbor Press, 2002), 168–197.
4. Nick Stinnett and John DeFrain, *Secrets of Strong Families* (New York: Berkley Books, 1985), 14.
5. Dolores Curran, cited in Charles M. Shelton, *Pastoral Counseling with Adolescents and Young Adults* (New York: Crossroad, 1995), 96–97.
6. Mary Pipher, *The Shelter of Each Other: Rebuilding Our Families* (New York: Grossett/Putnam, 1996), 230.
7. Stinnett and DeFrain, *Secrets of Strong Families,* 8.
8. Michael Riera, *Uncommon Sense for Parents with Teenagers* (Berkeley, Ca.: Celestial Arts, 1995), xiii.
9. Ibid., 4.
10. William Myers, *Theological Themes in Youth Ministry* (Cleveland: Pilgrim Press, 1987), xviii.
11. Walter Brueggemann, "Confirmation: Joining a Special Story," *Colloquy* (May/June 1974): 6–9.
12. William R. Myers, ed., *Becoming and Belonging: A Practical Design for Confirmation* (Cleveland: United Church Press, 1993), 13.
13. Robert L. Browning and Roy A. Reed, *Models of Confirmation and Baptismal Affirmation: Liturgical and Educational Issues and Designs* (Birmingham: Religious Education Press, 1995), 63–66.
14. James Wilde, "Rite of Christian Initiation of Adults: Some Pastoral Implications for Teens," *Confirmed as Children: Affirmed as Teens* (Chicago: Liturgy Training Publications, 1990), 59–60.